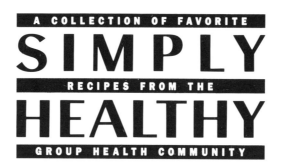

A COLLECTION OF FAVORITE

SIMPLY

RECIPES FROM THE

HEALTHY

GROUP HEALTH COMMUNITY

A COLLECTION OF FAVORITE
SIMPLY
RECIPES FROM THE
HEALTHY
GROUP HEALTH COMMUNITY

Foreword by Don A. Rogers, M.D.

Published by VIEW Publishing
Group Health Cooperative of Puget Sound
Seattle, Washington

Group
Health
Cooperative

Simply Healthy: A Collection of Favorite Recipes
from the Group Health Community

Cover design: Allen Woodard
Design: Margarite Hargrave
Illustrations: Jonathan Combs

Library of Congress Cataloging in Publication Data 89-83848

ISBN 0-9622912-0-X

First Edition

Printed in Canada

Contents

▲▲▲▲▲▲▲▲▲▲▲▲▲▲▲▲

Foreword

When the editors of "Simply Healthy" asked me to contribute to their timely and important project, I felt flattered and delighted. Perusing the text of the book, I found that the advice given here is consistent with the very precepts that have steered my career as a physician. I entered medical school because I wanted to help others. After medical school, I selected a residency in Family Practice because of my interest in families. I joined the Group Health Medical Staff because of the Cooperative's commitment to prevention. "Simply Healthy" is about all these precepts: It will help families prevent life-threatening illness.

In recent years, I have become increasingly convinced of the importance a healthy diet plays in the prevention of disease. In 1985, I was a member of the Group Health Nutritional Guideline Committee. With the help of Maureen Raskin, M.S., Ph.C., Ann P. Carter, M.D., and others, a set of nutritional guidelines for Group Health consumers was drafted. Since working on the Group Health Nutritional Guidelines, I have dramatically changed my eating habits, my family has improved their food selection patterns, and I have worked to raise public awareness about the importance of proper nutrition.

As I studied the medical and epidemiologic literature regarding nutrition and disease prevention, I was profoundly impressed with the potential health benefits of proper food selection. I learned that we live in the midst of an underacknowledged epidemic of premature and preventable deaths due to fat and cholesterol toxicity. I learned that heart disease and cancer are responsible for two-thirds of all deaths in the U.S., and that more Americans die of fat and cholesterol excess than from all other causes combined. But I also learned that heart disease is nutritionally preventable and many forms of cancer can be postponed. I became certain that the food choices we make each day have more influence on our personal life span than any other single factor.

We can solve the riddle of heart disease and we can lessen the number of premature deaths from cancer. Following the low-fat, high-fiber program described in "Simply Healthy" is the solution. It's time to start living that solution.

—*Don A. Rogers, M.D., Group Health Cooperative*

▲▲▲▲▲▲▲▲▲▲▲▲▲▲▲▲▲▲

Introduction

Welcome to *Simply Healthy: A Collection of Favorite Recipes from the Group Health Community*, a cookbook compiled for and by people interested in good food and good health. We hope the information and recipes in this book will help you discover that good food and good health form a natural partnership. You can put more of both into your life by learning more about food groups and keeping an open mind about how you cook.

You only have to take a quick glance at the cookbook section of your favorite bookstore to know that cooking has become an increasingly popular pastime. But it's not just the gourmet chefs who are gravitating toward the kitchen. Young adults and busy professionals trying to juggle classes, meetings, and work schedules are discovering that eating the right foods gives them the energy to cope with hectic lives. Young mothers and fathers bravely face the challenge of finding nutritious food for finicky preschoolers. Parents of teens wage war daily against the seemingly omnipotent influences of fast food and junk food. Retired seniors, some of them living on fixed incomes, work at getting the most nutrition their dollar can buy. And there are people of all ages doing their best to follow the doctor's orders: learning how to cook without salt or experimenting with recipes to see if one tablespoon of butter will work just as well as the four the recipe requires.

They're all heading for the kitchen with the best intentions, although sometimes they're armed more with determination than information. *Simply Healthy* is for all of them. In fact, it's for anyone who wants to eat a healthier diet—as simply as possible.

The more than 150 recipes that make up this book have been contributed by people who carefully created them for use in their own families. Recipes in *Simply Healthy* are original creations of Group Health Cooperative consumers—people who care about good health and good nutrition. Tested in homes and not in corporate test kitchens, these recipes have passed the toughest test of all: They're literally "family approved."

How did such a practical, grassroots guide to healthier eating come to be? The story of *Simply Healthy* is one of cooperation befitting Group Health Cooperative, the country's largest consumer-governed health maintenance organization.

▲▲▲▲▲▲▲▲▲▲▲▲▲▲▲▲▲

Editors of VIEW Magazine, the publication sent to all Group Health consumers, knew that nutrition concerns were important to their readers. Survey after survey told the editors a simple fact: Readers are hungry for information to improve their diets. At the same time, medical sources and research studies are continually pointing out the critical role diet plays in a wide range of health issues including weight control, high blood pressure, controlling cholesterol levels—even preventing cancer. The VIEW staff came up with a plan to educate readers about healthier eating while encouraging them to participate in a Cooperative-wide project with far-reaching benefits.

Beginning in July 1988 and concluding a year later, VIEW Magazine ran a series of educational stories focusing on food groups, including fruits, complex carbohydrates, dairy products, poultry and seafood, red meats, and vegetables. Group Health nutritionists provided up-to-date information about the foods: How much should be included in the daily diet, how it can best be prepared, what substitutions can be made for people who need to limit particular foods. All the information was designed to do one job—help people eat a balanc-ed, healthy diet and reduce the amount of fat, salt, and cholesterol they consume.

Readers were invited to experiment with new recipes—or to adapt old favorites to the healthier concepts they had just learned—and send their recipes to VIEW Magazine.

VIEW then arranged for Group Health nutritionists and dietitians to screen the recipes. Volunteers from throughout the organization prepared the dishes and still others participated in taste tests. Points were awarded in several categories including appearance, texture, and flavor. The highest scoring recipes are the ones you'll find in *Simply Healthy*. Finally, each recipe chosen to be part of the cookbook was put through a computerized nutritional analysis to determine the exact amounts of calories, fat, sodium, and cholesterol in each serving of each recipe.

The recipes in this book are the culmination of many people's best efforts toward better eating—truly a cooperative process in the name of good health and good taste. Enjoy.

Yours in good health, *The Editors*

▲▲▲▲▲▲▲▲▲▲▲▲▲▲▲▲▲▲

About this Cookbook

All the recipes in Simply Healthy have been screened by Group Health Cooperative nutritionists and analyzed for their nutritional value per serving. This analysis includes calories; the percentage of calories from fat; total grams of fat, protein, carbohydrates, dietary fiber; and milligrams of cholesterol.

The charts provided here give daily recommendations for each of these categories, based on information from the American Dietetic Association and the National Research Council of the National Academy of Sciences. These recommendations are for healthy people. If you have a disease or condition that requires a special therapeutic diet, please consult with your physician or nutritionist.

Recommended Calorie Ranges

Men		Women		Children	
Ages	**Calories**	**Ages**	**Calories**	**Ages**	**Calories**
11-14	2000-3700	11-14	1500-3000	1-3	900-1800
15-18	2100-3900	15-18	1200-3000	4-6	1300-2300
19-22	2500-3300	19-22	1700-2500	7-10	1650-3300
23-50	2300-3100	23-50	1600-2400		
51-75	2000-2800	51-75	1400-2200		
76+	1650-2450	76+	1200-2000		

Recommended Adult Nutritional Requirements

	MAXIMUM FAT	MINIMUM PROTEIN		MINIMUM CARBO- HYDRATES	MINIMUM FIBER	MAXIMUM CHOLESTEROL
		Men	Women			
1500 CALORIE DIET	50 g.	56 g.	44 g.	170 g.	25 g.	300 mg.
2000 CALORIE DIET	67 g.	56 g.	44 g.	225 g.	25 g.	300 mg.
2500 CALORIE DIET	83 g.	56 g.	44 g.	280 g.	25 g.	300 mg.

To further help you put this information in context, recipes also are marked with the following symbols to indicate their special dietary values:

Indicates that less than 30 percent of the total calories per serving is from fat and/or there are less than 10 grams of fat per serving. (Recommended daily intake is 30 percent of total calories.)

Indicates a sodium content of less than 300 milligrams per serving. (Recommended daily intake is 1,100 to 3,300 milligrams.)

Indicates less than 120 milligrams of cholesterol per serving. (Recommended daily intake is about 300 milligrams.)

Indicates 3 grams or more of dietary fiber per serving. (Recommended daily intake is 25 to 35 grams.)

The Group Health Cooperative nutritionists advise that a healthy diet can reduce your risk for heart disease, hypertension, cancer, and diabetes. If you have any of these conditions or diseases, a prudent diet often can improve your health or help you to prevent further complications.

The dietary guidelines provided below can help you prevent or control certain diseases or conditions:

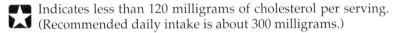

HEART DISEASE	HYPERTENSION	CANCER	DIABETES
low fat	low fat	low fat	low fat
low sodium	low sodium		
low cholesterol	low cholesterol		low cholesterol
high fiber	high fiber	high fiber	high fiber

As you can see, the heart symbol is particularly significant because a low-fat diet is important in the prevention and management of all these diseases and conditions. The nutritionists recommend that recipes without the heart symbol be used judiciously.

Fruit

◆

▲▲▲▲▲▲▲▲▲▲▲▲▲▲▲▲▲▲▲

Fruit

In these health-conscious times, we're all searching for the ultimate wonder food we can consume without guilt: something that tastes great and is good for us, too. It should be low in fat, low in cholesterol, low in sodium, and high in fiber. Well, call off the search and take another look at fruit. Bite into a crisp apple. Taste a juicy orange or pop a couple of ripe strawberries into your mouth. These are wonder foods: They're low in fat, calories, and sodium, and are good sources of fiber. And best of all, their great sweet tastes make them realistic alternatives to those less healthy, chocolatey concoctions that leap to mind whenever a sweet tooth shifts into overdrive.

Given the convenience and satisfying sweetness of many fruits, it's not surprising that Americans like to eat fruit between or after meals. A recent national survey revealed that 43 percent of the people surveyed said that snack time is when they most often eat fresh fruit. As a snack, fruit has a lot going for it: It's easy to tote, filling, and requires no preparation or refrigeration. Packing an apple for a midmorning snack might help you pass up the apple Danish during your coffee break.

But don't limit fruit to snack time. Once you decide to add more fruit to your daily diet, you'll discover just how versatile fruit can be. Add a whole orange to your breakfast. Try a fruit salad with yogurt for lunch, or finish your midday meal with a bunch of grapes. After dinner, try some cantaloupe with frozen yogurt or sherbet instead of the butter pound cake.

A few changes like these, made simply and consistently, can make a big difference in your health. You'll be adding fiber and nutrients to your diet while reducing your intake of fats and refined sugars. And, best of all, you'll still be able to satisfy your craving for something sweet.

The number-one thing to remember about fruit is that the less you do to it, the better it is for you. Always include some fresh, uncooked fruit in your diet because cooking destroys some vitamins and minerals. And when you do cook fruit, be careful what you add to it. Recipes that start with fruit and add cups of sugar, honey, or other sweeteners can quickly turn an ideal snack food into dietary disaster.

▲▲▲▲▲▲▲▲▲▲▲▲▲▲▲▲▲

Nutritionists recommend using unsweetened fruit juice in combination with fresh fruits in recipes whenever possible. The fruit juice adds even more vitamins to the fruit without adding sugar.

Except for very young children who may have trouble chewing the skin on fruits, most people will benefit from not peeling fruits such as apples, peaches, and pears. There's a good supply of vitamins, minerals and fiber in that peel that will be put to much better use in your body than in the garbage disposal. Be sure to wash the fruit well before you eat it.

Similarly, you'll get more fiber—and a more satisfied feeling—by eating a whole orange instead of drinking orange juice. A whole apple with peel, for example, provides two grams of fiber while a half cup of applesauce provides 0.65 gram of fiber, and three-quarters of a cup of apple juice supplies only 0.25 gram of fiber.

If you eat a lot of dried fruits, be aware that some drying processes use large amounts of sodium. Also, remember that calories and the natural sugar content are more concentrated in dried fruits because the water has been removed. This means that you're getting more calories in a half cup of dried apricots than in whole fresh apricots.

When you shop, take some time and care and follow these tips from the Washington State University Cooperative Extension office:

◆ Select fresh fruits that have no signs of bruising.

◆ Use fresh fruits quickly to prevent spoilage and waste.

◆ Serve fruits quickly after cutting them to prevent vitamin loss.

And when you're ready to get creative, try some of the following delicious, healthy, fresh fruit recipes from the Group Health community.

Apple-Berry Butter

SUE BILLINGSLEY, SEATTLE

Makes 24 - 1 tablespoon servings

2 tart apples, about 2 cups diced
1 cup ripe blackberries
1/3 to 1/2 cup sugar
1/4 to 1/3 cup water

Wash apples and cut into small pieces, core and all. Add water. Bring to a boil, then lower heat, cover pan, and simmer until apples are soft and tender. Check occasionally, adding more water if needed. Add blackberries to apples and continue to cook until berries are soft.

Remove pan from heat and cool. Press fruit mixture through a sieve into a deep saucepan. Add sugar and cook, stirring frequently, until mixture is thick and no longer runny. (It will thicken a bit more when refrigerated.) Spread on toast or muffins.

Nutritional Analysis (per serving)

Calories 24.5	Carbohydrates ...... 6.31 g
Calories from fat 2%	Dietary fiber ...... 0.634 g
Total fat ...... 0.056 g	Cholesterol ...... 0 mg
Protein.. ...... 0.061 g	Sodium ...... 0.021 mg

Berry Pie

AMY GLENN, SUMNER

Serves 8

1 8-inch graham cracker crust
4 1/2 cups blueberries, raspberries, or sliced
   strawberries
3/4 cup granulated sugar
3 tablespoons cornstarch
3 tablespoons lemon juice
1 pound low fat cottage cheese
1/2 teaspoon ground cinnamon
1 teaspoon vanilla

In blender, combine 2 cups berries with 1/2 cup sugar, cornstarch, and lemon juice. Cook until clear and thick. Cool. Add 2 cups fresh berries. Pour into crust. In blender, combine cottage cheese, cinnamon, 1/4 cup sugar, and vanilla. Spread over berry filling. Chill.

Nutritional Analysis (per serving)

Calories 372	Carbohydrates ...... 59.4 g
Calories from fat 28%	Dietary fiber ...... 2.69 g
Total fat ...... 11.8 g	Cholesterol ...... 2.51 mg
Protein.. ...... 9.31 g	Sodium ...... 474 mg

Cranappetizer

MARVA J. DAWN, VANCOUVER, WA

Serves 16

1 package whole cranberries
3 cups apple pieces, skins can be left on
1/2 cup raisins
1 teaspoon cinnamon
1/2 teaspoon nutmeg
1/2 teaspoon ginger
1/2 teaspoon cloves
sugar substitute to equal 1/2 cup sugar,
   or to taste
1 cup water

Boil water with sugar substitute in large kettle. Add cranberries and continue boiling until berries start to pop. Add apples and simmer until apples are almost tender. Add raisins and spices to taste. Serve warm for appetizer, or as a side for chicken or turkey meat loaf.

Nutritional Analysis (per serving)

Calories 40.1	Carbohydrates ...... 10.5 g
Calories from fat 4%	Dietary fiber ...... 1.87 g
Total fat ...... 0.192 g	Cholesterol ...... 0 mg
Protein.. ...... 0.317 g	Sodium ...... 1.08 mg

Cranberry Waldorf Salad

AMY GLENN, SUMNER

Serves 8

1 1/2 cups cranberries, chopped
1 cup unpeeled apples, chopped
1/2 cup celery, chopped

1 cup seedless grapes, halved
¹/₂ cup walnuts, chopped
¹/₄ teaspoon cinnamon
1 8-ounce carton low fat vanilla yogurt

Combine cranberries, apples, celery, grapes and walnuts. Add cinnamon to yogurt. Fold yogurt into fruit and coat. Chill. Garnish with a sprig of frozen grapes.

Nutritional Analysis (per serving)

Calories	105	Carbohydrates	13.4 g
Calories from fat	42%	Dietary fiber	1.86 g
Total fat	5.20 g	Cholesterol	1.42 mg
Protein..	2.75 g	Sodium	26.8 mg

Dena's Plum Sauce

ELDEENA DAVIS, PUYALLUP

Makes 6 ¹/₄-cup servings

1 ¹/₂ cups plums
4 large cloves, minced
1 ¹/₂ tablespoon sugar
salt to taste
freshly ground pepper to taste

In a blender or food processor puree 1 ¹/₂ pounds of plums. Put puree in a sauce pan and add garlic, salt and pepper. Bring to boil. Reduce heat and simmer for 5 minutes, stirring frequently.

Excellent as a sauce for beef fondue or, when broiling or barbecuing, as a basting sauce for all meat. Serve at room temperature when used as a sauce. Freezes well.

Nutritional Analysis (per serving)

Calories	37.8	Carbohydrates	9.15 g
Calories from fat	6%	Dietary fiber	0.833 g
Total fat	0.265 g	Cholesterol	0 mg
Protein..	0.452 g	Sodium	0.668 mg

Easy & Healthy Blueberry Cobbler

BETTY FITZGERALD, BELLEVUE

Serves 8

²/₃ cup flour
¹/₂ cup sugar
3 teaspoons low sodium baking powder
²/₃ cup skimmed milk
2 tablespoons low cholesterol margarine
2 cups blueberries (thawed, if frozen)
1 cup nonfat frozen yogurt, vanilla or wildberry flavor

In bowl blend together flour, sugar, and baking powder. Add milk and stir. Melt the margarine in deep 1- to 1 ¹/₂-quart casserole. Pour in batter and sprinkle evenly with blueberries. Bake for 40 to 45 minutes, or until top is lightly browned, at 350 degrees. Top each serving with a dollop of frozen yogurt.

Nutritional Analysis (per serving)

Calories	172	Carbohydrates	32.3 g
Calories from fat	13%	Dietary fiber	1.29 g
Total fat	2.55 g	Cholesterol	1.37 mg
Protein..	5.52 g	Sodium	93.1 mg

Fresh Fruit Cocktail with Mint Sauce

VIRGINIA MALICO, SPOKANE

Serves 8

One bunch fresh, washed mint
1 cup sugar
¹/₂ cup water
1 to 2 tablespoons lemon juice
4 cups seasonal fruit: watermelon, cantaloupe, grapes, berries, or other fruit in season.

Combine sugar and water in a saucepan. Bring to boil on stove or in microwave. Remove from heat. Draw four mint sprigs through mixture several times. Add lemon juice and cool. Serve 2 tablespoons of sauce over ¹/₂ cup servings of fruit. Top with remaining sprigs of mint.

Nutritional Analysis (per serving)

Calories	101	Carbohydrates	26.1 g
Calories from fat	0%	Dietary fiber	0.183 g
Total fat	0.010 g	Cholesterol	0 mg
Protein..	0.074 g	Sodium	0.688 mg

Frosty Strawberry Squares

JUDY RAINWATER, KIRKLAND

Serves 12

1 cup flour
2 tablespoons melted butter
2 tablespoons brown sugar
2 egg whites
$^1/_2$ cup sugar
2 tablespoons lemon juice
1 $^1/_2$ cup partially frozen unsweetened fruit
$^1/_4$ cup chopped nuts

Mix the flour, butter and brown sugar and spread in a 9-x-13-inch pan. Bake for 7 to 10 minutes at 350 degrees. Set aside to cool.

Place the egg whites, sugar, lemon juice and partially thawed fruit in mixing bowl and beat until stiff peaks form, about 10 minutes. Spread on top of the crumb layer, sprinkle with chopped nuts. Freeze for at least 6 hours.

Nutritional Analysis (per serving)

Calories	121	Carbohydrates	21.0 g
Calories from fat	25%	Dietary fiber	1.09 g
Total fat	3.46 g	Cholesterol	5.18 mg
Protein..	2.30 g	Sodium	10.7 mg

Fruit Crispy

CHERYL A. COLEMAN, SHELTON

Serves 6

4 cups fruit, any kind, fresh or frozen
1 tablespoon unbleached flour, more or less depending on juiciness of fruit

3 tablespoons brown sugar, or to taste
1 $^1/_2$ teaspoons cinnamon
$^1/_2$ cup oat bran
$^1/_2$ cup unbleached flour
1 cup soft margarine, melted
4 tablespoons fruit juice or water

In 10-inch pie dish, gently toss 1 tablespoon of flour, $^1/_2$ teaspoon cinnamon and 1 tablespoon brown sugar with fruit. Mix together remaining ingredients except fruit juice. Spread over fruit, covering completely. Sprinkle with fruit juice. Bake at 400 degrees for 30 to 40 minutes or until brown and bubbly.

Nutritional Analysis (per serving)

Calories	191	Carbohydrates	39.7 g
Calories from fat	19%	Dietary fiber	4.72 g
Total fat	4.56 g	Cholesterol	0 mg
Protein..	3.72 g	Sodium	158 mg

Fruit Soup

BEVERLY SMITH, FERNDALE

Serves 8

1 10-ounce package frozen raspberries
1 10-ounce package frozen blueberries
2 cups frozen blackberries, loganberries, or boysenberries
1 8-ounce package dried prunes, pitted or unpitted, or 1 6-ounce package diced dried fruit bits
1 cup orange juice
1 tablespoon minute tapioca
$^1/_4$ cup sugar
$^1/_4$ teaspoon cinnamon
whipped cream, if desired

Soften tapioca in orange juice for 5 minutes in a saucepan. Add all fruits, thawed or unthawed, sugar, and cinnamon. Heat to boiling. Simmer for 10 minutes to cook tapioca and prunes. Remove from heat and cool. When temperature is reduced to warm, serve in dessert dishes, with a dollop of whipped cream if desired. Can also be served cool the next day.

Nutritional Analysis (per serving)

Calories 274	Carbohydrates .... 48.1 g
Calories from fat 31%	Dietary fiber .... 7.23 g
Total fat .... 9.95 g	Cholesterol .... 33.4 mg
Protein.. .... 2.51 g	Sodium .... 15.2 mg

Gorties
(Fruit Smoothie)

M. Jolene Ramaker, Corvallis, Ore.

Serves 4

*1 cup whole frozen strawberries,
   unsweetened
1 cup apple juice, cold, unsweetened
1 small ripe banana, peeled
1 cup nonfat plain yogurt*

Place all ingredients in blender. Blend at high speed. Pour into chilled glasses.

Nutritional Analysis (per serving)

Calories 108	Carbohydrates .... 23.8 g
Calories from fat 3%	Dietary fiber .... 1.81 g
Total fat .... 0.392 g	Cholesterol .... 1.00 mg
Protein.. .... 3.83 g	Sodium .... 46.1 mg

Mango & Friends Salad

Enid L. Ostrander, Seattle

Serves 4

*1 ripe mango, peel and cut into bite size
   pieces
1/2 large cantaloupe, cut into bite size pieces
1 pint strawberries, stem and cut large
   berries in half
1 8 1/4-ounce can of tidbit pineapple, drained
1/2 cup low fat strawberry yogurt*

Mix fruits together lightly. Add strawberry yogurt. Stir until fruit mixture is lightly coated.

Nutritional Analysis (per serving)

Calories 139	Carbohydrates .... 32.9 g
Calories from fat 6%	Dietary fiber .... 5.04 g
Total fat .... 0.978 g	Cholesterol .... 1.25 mg
Protein.. .... 2.76 g	Sodium .... 24.3 mg

Medicine Lake Wild Raspberry & Cantaloupe Dessert

Jan Bogle, Seattle

Serves 4

*1 large cantaloupe
2 cups lime sherbet
1 1/2 cups raspberries
kiwi fruit slices for garnish, optional*

Use good quality, well ripened fruit for natural sweetness. Quarter cantaloupe, remove seeds.

Place 1/2 cup lime sherbet on each serving. Sprinkle 1/4 to 1/3 cup raspberries on scoop of sherbet. Sliced kiwi fruit makes an attractive garnish if desired.

Nutritional Analysis (per serving)

Calories 204	Carbohydrates .... 45.8 g
Calories from fat 11%	Dietary fiber .... 4.21 g
Total fat .... 2.54 g	Cholesterol .... 7.00 mg
Protein.. .... 2.67 g	Sodium .... 56.0 mg

Microwave Applesauce Chunks

Phoebe N. Hagler, Bellevue

Serves 8

*8 cups tart apples, peeled and sliced
1/3 cup sugar
1 teaspoon cinnamon
1/2 teaspoon nutmeg
1/2 cup water*

Fill 2-quart glass casserole with apples. Sprinkle with sugar and spice mix. Pour in water. Cover with wax paper. Microwave 8 minutes on high, or until apples are slightly tender. Stir halfway through cooking time. Let stand 5 minutes. Serve warm or chilled.

Nutritional Analysis (per serving)

Calories 97.5	Carbohydrates .... 25.3 g
Calories from fat 4%	Dietary fiber .... 2.76 g
Total fat .... 0.443 g	Cholesterol .... 0 mg
Protein.. .... 0.219 g	Sodium .... 0.234 mg

Nectarines and Kiwi with Almond Yogurt Topping

Cynthia Stroo, Duvall

Serves 6

3 nectarines
3 kiwis
$^1/_2$ cup low fat unflavored yogurt
2 tablespoons honey
1 teaspoon almond extract
pinch of ground cinnamon
4 mint sprigs for garnish

Peel, pit and slice nectarines. Toss with 1 tablespoon of the honey and pinch of ground cinnamon. Pare kiwis and slice crosswise. Arrange kiwi slices on each of 6 chilled plates. Arrange nectarine slices on top of kiwis.

Mix yogurt with almond extract and remaining 1 tablespoon of honey. Dollop the yogurt mixture in center of fruit composition and garnish with small sprigs of mint.

Nutritional Analysis (per serving)

Calories 79.7	Carbohydrates .... 18.0 g
Calories from fat 8%	Dietary fiber .... 2.67 g
Total fat .... 0.774 g	Cholesterol .... 1.17 mg
Protein.. .... 2.02 g	Sodium .... 15.5 mg

Nutty Fruit Salad

Connie McGarry, Bothell

Serves 10

$^3/_4$ cup peanuts, no skins
$^1/_2$ cup sunflower seeds
1 cup apples, sliced or cubed
1 cup bananas, sliced
$^1/_2$ cup tangerines
1 cup fresh pineapple tidbits
1 cup seedless green grapes
$^1/_2$ cup raisins
$^1/_4$ cup shredded coconut
3 to 4 tablespoons honey
juice of $^1/_2$ lemon
$^1/_2$ cup pineapple juice

Combine all ingredients in a large bowl and mix thoroughly in order given. Serve in fruit compote dish. May add a dollop of any flavor low fat yogurt on top when ready to serve.

Nutritional Analysis (per serving)

Calories 215	Carbohydrates .... 30.2 g
Calories from fat 39%	Dietary fiber .... 3.55 g
Total fat .... 10.1 g	Cholesterol .... 0.063 mg
Protein.. .... 5.34 g	Sodium .... 11.1 mg

Peach Nut Cake

Pat Bretheim, Kirkland

Serves 8

Cake ingredients

1 $^1/_2$ cups whole wheat flour
1 teaspoon baking powder
$^1/_4$ teaspoon salt
$^1/_2$ teaspoon cinnamon
1 cup brown sugar
2 eggs
$^1/_2$ cup oil
1 teaspoon vanilla
$^1/_2$ 14-ounce can drained peach slices
1 cup cashews or walnuts

Glaze ingredients

1 tablespoon margarine
2 tablespoons honey

¹/₂ 14-ounce can drained peach slices

Spray glass deep-dish pan with non-stick cooking spray. Cook glaze ingredients on stovetop for 5 to 10 minutes and pour liquid part of glaze into the glass dish, retaining peach slices until glaze cools slightly, then arranging them in a pinwheel pattern. You may decorate the cake by placing extra nuts between the peach slices. Set aside.

Mix the whole wheat flour, baking powder, salt, cinnamon and brown sugar. In a separate bowl, beat together eggs, oil, vanilla and remainder of peach slices. Slowly add in flour mixture. With a large spoon, fold in nuts.

Spoon dough into glass dish, taking care not to disturb the pinwheel design. Bake 35 to 45 minutes or until a toothpick inserted in the center comes out clean.

Cool 5 minutes, then invert onto a plate before the glaze gets sticky. If peach slices are loose, rearrange into their places. Delicious warm or cool.

Nutritional Analysis (per serving)

Calories 463	Carbohydrates .... 54.9 g
Calories from fat 48%	Dietary fiber .... 4.32 g
Total fat .... 25.6 g	Cholesterol .... 52.0 mg
Protein.. .... 8.76 g	Sodium .... 116 mg

Rhubarb Crunch

DIANE WRAY, ARLINGTON

Serves 8

1 cup whole wheat flour
³/₄ cup rolled oats, regular or quick
²/₃ cup brown sugar, packed
¹/₂ cup margarine, melted
¹/₂ cup wheat germ, raw
1 teaspoon cinnamon
¹/₂ cup sugar
3 tablespoons cornstarch
1 cup apple juice
1 teaspoon vanilla extract
4 cups rhubarb, diced

Mix flour, oats, brown sugar, wheat germ, margarine, and cinnamon until crumbly. Press ¹/₂ of mixture into greased 9-inch square glass baking dish.

Mix sugar and cornstarch. Stir in apple juice. Cook in saucepan on stovetop, or in dish in microwave, until thickened and clear, stirring frequently. Stir in vanilla extract. Spread diced rhubarb over crumb mixture in 9 inch dish. Pour thickened sauce over rhubarb and top with remaining crumbs. Bake for one hour at 325 degrees. Serve warm or cool.

Nutritional Analysis (per serving)

Calories 337	Carbohydrates .... 59.5 g
Calories from fat 26%	Dietary fiber .... 5.16 g
Total fat .... 10.1 g	Cholesterol .... 0 mg
Protein.. .... 5.14 g	Sodium .... 155 mg

Rum-Orange Bananas

SHEILA BRAWITT, EVERETT

Serves 4

2 tablespoons unsalted margarine
5 tablespoons light rum
¹/₄ cup fresh orange juice
3 tablespoons brown sugar, firmly packed
¹/₄ teaspoon freshly grated nutmeg
4 firm ripe bananas, peeled and halved
*   lengthwise*

Melt margarine in a non-stick skillet over low heat. Add 3 tablespoons rum, orange juice, brown sugar and nutmeg. Simmer until slightly thickened, 1 to 2 minutes. Add bananas and turn to coat. Add remaining 2 tablespoons of rum. Heat and ignite, shaking skillet gently until flames subside. Serve hot.

Nutritional Analysis (per serving)

Calories 176	Carbohydrates .... 38.3 g
Calories from fat 16%	Dietary fiber .... 2.37 g
Total fat .... 3.38 g	Cholesterol .... 0 mg
Protein.. .... 1.33 g	Sodium .... 73.8 mg

Strawberry Angel Food Trifle

Roberta Krause, Redmond

Serves 12

1 box angel food cake mix
1 1.6-ounce package instant sugar-free
  vanilla pudding mix
1 ¹/₂ cups low fat milk
2 8-ounce cartons low fat strawberry yogurt
1 package whipped topping mix
1 to 1 ¹/₂ quarts fresh strawberries, stemmed
  and sliced
¹/₃ cup slivered almonds, toasted

Bake angel food cake and slice very thin, into approximately 36 slices. Combine pudding mix, milk, and yogurt. Make whipped topping, using nonfat or lowfat milk.

In a large, deep, glass serving dish, put the cake together as follows: one layer of cake slices, using approximately 12 slices; ¹/₃ of pudding mixture, spread evenly; ¹/₃ of topping mixture, spread evenly; ¹/₂ of strawberries; ¹/₃ of almonds. Repeat this sequence once.

Assemble final layer with 12 cake slices, pudding, topping, and remaining almonds. Refrigerate several hours or overnight.

Nutritional Analysis (per serving)

Calories 246	Carbohydrates .... 45.6 g
Calories from fat 15%	Dietary fiber .... 1.97 g
Total fat .... 4.27 g	Cholesterol .... 3.83 mg
Protein.. .... 8.08 g	Sodium .... 340 mg

Strawberry Meringues

Amy Glenn, Sumner

Serves 8

1 teaspoon vinegar
3 egg whites, at room temperature
1 teaspoon cold water

¹/₂ teaspoon vanilla extract
¹/₂ teaspoon baking powder
¹/₈ teaspoon salt
1 cup sugar
1 cup sliced strawberries
¹/₂ cup low fat vanilla yogurt

Combine egg whites, water, vinegar, vanilla, baking powder and salt in large mixing bowl. Beat until frothy. Gradually add sugar, 1 tablespoon at a time until stiff peaks form. Spoon into 8 equal mounds on baking sheet lined with brown paper. Shape with spoon into shells with sides 1-inch high.

Bake for 1 hour at 250 degrees. Cool away from drafts. Remove from paper. May be stored in plastic bag in refrigerator. Fill with sliced strawberries 1 hour before serving. Garnish with yogurt.

Nutritional Analysis (per serving)

Calories 120	Carbohydrates .... 28.4 g
Calories from fat 2%	Dietary fiber .... 0.484 g
Total fat .... 0.246 g	Cholesterol .... 0.712 mg
Protein.. .... 2.07 g	Sodium .... 62.3 mg

Strawberry Pie

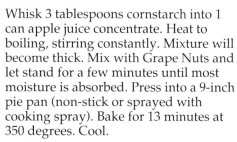

Kimberly Bunten, Kirkland

Serves 8

5 tablespoons cornstarch
2 6-ounce apple juice concentrate
1 ¹/₂ cups Grape Nuts cereal
5 cups fresh strawberries
¹/₄ cup cold water

Whisk 3 tablespoons cornstarch into 1 can apple juice concentrate. Heat to boiling, stirring constantly. Mixture will become thick. Mix with Grape Nuts and let stand for a few minutes until most moisture is absorbed. Press into a 9-inch pie pan (non-stick or sprayed with cooking spray). Bake for 13 minutes at 350 degrees. Cool.

Mash 2 cups of strawberries. Add ¹/₃ cup

apple juice concentrate. Whisk 2 tablespoons cornstarch into cold water and pour into mashed fruit and juice mixture. Heat to boiling, stirring constantly. Mixture will become a thick, shiny glaze. Fill pie crust with remaining whole strawberries. Pour glaze over the top. Chill and serve.

Nutritional Analysis (per serving)

Calories 176	Carbohydrates .... 41.9 g
Calories from fat 3%	Dietary fiber .... 3.96 g
Total fat .... 0.578 g	Cholesterol .... 0 mg
Protein.. .... 3.23 g	Sodium .... 158 mg

Stuffed Peaches

M. VOLKMANN, BALLARD

Serves 6

1 green pepper
4 celery hearts
¹/₂ cup blanched almonds
3 tablespoons low calorie mayonnaise
3 melba peaches, in halves

Put vegetables and nuts through meat grinder or food processor. Moisten with mayonnaise. Form into balls and put one ball into each peach half.

Nutritional Analysis (per serving)

Calories 114	Carbohydrates .... 9.88 g
Calories from fat 58%	Dietary fiber .... 2.75 g
Total fat .... 7.92 g	Cholesterol .... 1.81 mg
Protein.. .... 3.07 g	Sodium .... 62.2 mg

Summertime Berry Pie

TERRI DUEVER, BELFAIR

Serves 8

Crust

1 ¹/₂ cups graham cracker crumbs
2 tablespoons honey, microwaved 15 seconds on high

1 tablespoon cooking oil
¹/₄ teaspoon cinnamon

Filling

1 envelope unflavored gelatin
¹/₄ cup nonfat evaporated milk
2 tablespoons honey
dash of salt
1 cup low fat plain yogurt
¹/₂ teaspoon vanilla
4 cups fresh blueberries or blackberries
¹/₄ cup sugar
2 tablespoons corn starch

Combine graham cracker crumbs, honey, cooking oil, and cinnamon. Pat graham cracker mixture into 9-inch pie pan. Bake for 10 minutes at 350 degrees. Cool.

Mix gelatin in 2 tablespoons of water. Set aside. Microwave evaporated milk for 1 minute on high. Add honey, salt, and gelatin mixture. Stir until smooth. Add yogurt and vanilla. Whisk until smooth. Pour into cooled crust and refrigerate until soft set, approximately 30 minutes.

Combine 1 ¹/₂ cups berries with sugar. Microwave on high for 3 minutes. Stir and mash with potato masher. Combine corn starch with 2 tablespoons water. Add to mashed berry mixture. Microwave on high for 1 minute. Stir.

Arrange 2 ¹/₂ cups raw berries on top of yogurt mixture. Pour mashed berry mixture evenly over top. Refrigerate until set, approximately 2 hours. Serve.

Nutritional Analysis (per serving)

Calories 243	Carbohydrates .... 47.1 g
Calories from fat 17%	Dietary fiber .... 5.59 g
Total fat .... 4.80 g	Cholesterol .... 2.06 mg
Protein.. .... 5.07 g	Sodium .... 169 mg

Surprise Apple-Cabbage Salad

AMY GLENN, SUMNER

Serves 6

1 3-ounce package lemon gelatin
1 $^2/_3$ cup boiling water
3 tablespoon vinegar
1 tablespoon granulated sugar
$^1/_2$ cup diced unpeeled apples
$^1/_4$ cup raisins
1 cup shredded cabbage
$^1/_4$ teaspoon paprika

Dissolve gelatin in boiling water. Add vinegar and sugar. Cool until slightly thickened. Add rest of ingredients. Pour into 1-quart mold or 8-inch square pan. Chill and serve on lettuce leaf. Garnish with radish rose and parsley.

Nutritional Analysis (per serving)

Calories	46.7	Carbohydrates	12.1 g
Calories from fat	2%	Dietary fiber	0.945 g
Total fat	0.088 g	Cholesterol	0 mg
Protein..	0.699 g	Sodium	12.8 mg

Tofu Pie with Blueberry Sauce

LESLIE THISTLE, NEWMAN LAKE

Serves 8

Crust

16 graham crackers
$^1/_2$ cup oil
1 teaspoon honey

Filling

8 ounces neufchatel cheese
$^1/_2$ pound drained tofu
4 large egg whites
$^3/_4$ cup honey
2 tablespoons vanilla
6 tablespoons powdered milk

Topping

2 cups low fat yogurt
1$^1/_2$ teaspoons vanilla
2 tablespoons honey

Hot Blueberry Sauce

2 cups blueberries
$^1/_2$ cup honey
1$^1/_2$ tablespoons lemon juice
1$^1/_2$ heaping tablespoons cornstarch
$^1/_4$ cup water

Roll or crush graham crackers. Mix with oil and honey. Press into a 10-inch pie plate. Chill 1 hour.

For filling, blend tofu with powdered milk, vanilla, and egg whites. With electric mixer, whip cream cheese until fluffy. Slowly add tofu mixture to cheese and mix until smooth. Pour filling into pie shell. Bake at 300 degrees for about 30 to 40 minutes, or until custard will not stick to your finger when lightly touched.

Mix together topping ingredients and spread over baked pie. Return pie to oven for another 5 to 10 minutes. Chill pie several hours before serving. Serve with hot blueberry sauce.

To make sauce, boil berries, honey, lemon, and water. Dissolve cornstarch in a little water. Stir into blueberries until thick.

Nutritional Analysis (per serving)

Calories	537	Carbohydrates	73.3 g
Calories from fat	39%	Dietary fiber	1.69 g
Total fat	24.2 g	Cholesterol	26.0 mg
Protein..	12.3 g	Sodium	289 mg

Complex Carbohydrates

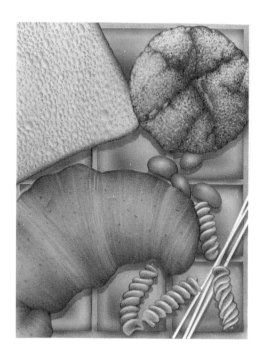

▲▲▲▲▲▲▲▲▲▲▲▲▲▲▲▲▲▲▲

Complex Carbohydrates

Did you grow up thinking that beans were what people ate when they couldn't afford meat? Did you suffer through years of dieting when you allowed yourself to eat one piece of bread a day and avoided pasta and potatoes? You'll be glad to know that breads, beans, and pastas—especially those high in fiber—are being acknowledged by doctors, nutritionists, and dietitians as the dietary jewels of the 1990s.

In fact, the American Heart Association recommends that all Americans substitute complex carbohydrates for some of the protein—and much of the fat—in their diets. Current guidelines call for a diet that derives 50 to 55 percent of its calories from carbohydrates, not more than 30 percent from fat and approximately 15 percent from protein.

For a 2,000-calorie daily diet, the new recommendations translate into 10 servings of starchy foods; four servings of nonstarchy vegetables; four fruits; six ounces of meat, fish, or poultry; and two cups of nonfat milk.

Note that the carbohydrates you want are high-fiber complex carbohydrates, the kind found in vegetables, fruits, beans, grains, and breads—not simple carbohydrates found in honey and table sugar.

Carbohydrates are the most efficient energy source around. They are easier to digest than proteins or fats, and they leave the digestive tract faster to travel to other parts of the body. Any excess carbohydrate is stored as energy reserve, a fact athletes exploit when they load up on carbohydrates before a race.

Complex carbohydrates are often high in fiber—the indigestible part of plants. Fiber takes up space and absorbs water. It makes you feel fuller so you feel more satisfied.

Evidence shows that certain soluble fibers such as pectin in apples and oat bran help lower cholesterol and glucose levels in the blood. Lowered cholesterol levels can mean decreased risk for heart attacks. The American Cancer Society also recommends a diet high in fiber because some studies suggest that fiber may help reduce the risk of colon cancer.

In addition, complex carbohydrates are a good source of vitamins and minerals.

So the switch to carbos is on. But a lot of re-education will be needed before people start revamping their diets. Dieters often shy away from starches, believing them to be fattening. But take a look at the facts: A five-ounce portion of steak contains 550 calories. Five ounces of rice is 154 calories, five ounces of pasta is 210 and five ounces of bread (approximately five slices) is 390.

It's not the carbohydrate food that is fattening; it's what people put on it or in it when they're cooking and baking that adds the extra calories. Potatoes and pasta are good for you. But butter, sour cream, and Alfredo sauce are not. Try topping pasta with steamed vegetables instead. Or try yogurt on your baked potato instead of butter.

Other ways to add complex carbohydrates to your diet:

◆ Begin the day with a whole-grain cereal or bread, low-fat milk, and a piece of fruit.

◆ At lunch, make a sandwich with whole-grain bread, adding lots of alfalfa sprouts, shredded carrots, or cucumbers. Skimp on meat, and use low fat chicken or turkey. Skip the cheese. Or try bean or vegetable soup, low-calorie yogurt, or a salad bar (skimp on cheese, ham, and salad dressing).

◆ Fill up on starchy foods such as corn, pasta, potatoes, and brown rice, and limit meat portions to two to three ounces per serving. In fact, try viewing the meat as a side dish to a primarily vegetarian entree, or forego meat altogether at least once a week.

◆ Substitute whole-wheat flour for up to one-half of the white flour in recipes whenever possible.

Take a look at the following recipes for ideas on how to cook the healthy, high-carbo way.

Barbara's Banana Bran Muffins

BARBARA REID, SEATTLE

Makes 12 to 18 muffins

2 cups whole-wheat flour
1 ¹/₂ cups oat bran
dash salt
1 ¹/₄ teaspoon baking soda
1 cup nonfat milk
1 cup low fat plain yogurt
1 egg, beaten
¹/₂ cup molasses
2 to 4 tablespoons melted corn-oil margarine
1 cup mashed banana (2 medium bananas)

Spray muffin tins with non-stick cooking spray.

Stir together flour, bran, salt, and soda. Set aside. Beat milk, yogurt, egg, molasses, and melted margarine. Stir in banana. Add flour mixture to milk mixture, stirring only a few times until dry ingredients are almost moist. Add raisins and stir until they are distributed. Mixture should not be smooth; overmixing may cause dry texture.

Fill muffin tins ²/₃ to ³/₄ full. Bake at 350 degrees for 25 minutes, or until finger leaves slight indentation when muffins are touched. Cool in tins for 5 to 10 minutes.

Nutritional Analysis (per serving)

Calories	138	
Calories from fat	17%	
Total fat	2.92 g	
Protein	5.41 g	
Carbohydrates	27.2 g	
Dietary fiber	3.60 g	
Cholesterol	14.1 mg	
Sodium	104 mg	

Better than Store Bought Beans

SHEILA BROWITT, EVERETT

Serves 8

2 cups pinto beans
1 pound ground chicken or turkey
¹/₂ cup molasses
¹/₂ cup brown sugar
2 medium onions, chopped
1 ¹/₂ cups low sodium tomato juice
1 cup unsalted, cooked carrot rounds
¹/₂ teaspoon pepper
¹/₂ teaspoon unsalted chili powder
¹/₂ teaspoon dry mustard

Soak beans overnight in cold water. Drain. Add water to cover, bring to a boil, and simmer until tender. Drain.

Brown chicken or turkey in a non-stick skillet. Place beans in a bean cooker along with all other ingredients. Stir well. Bring to a boil and turn down to simmer or bake for 1 to 1 ¹/₂ hours (or until beans are tender) at 350 degrees. Additional unsalted tomato juice may be needed.

Nutritional Analysis (per serving)

Calories	402	Carbohydrates	64.2 g
Calories from fat	10%	Dietary fiber	16.4 g
Total fat	4.67 g	Cholesterol	47.0 mg
Protein	27.0 g	Sodium	70.9 mg

Black Gold

TOM DE GROOT, SEATTLE

Serves 6

1 cup black beans, uncooked
3 tablespoons olive oil
1 medium onion, chopped
4 cloves garlic, minced
1 green pepper, chopped
2 tablespoons mild chili powder
¹/₂ teaspoon cumin
¹/₄ teaspoon black pepper
1 28-ounce can tomatoes, chopped

2 cups water
$^1/_2$ teaspoon salt
1 tablespoon brown sugar
dash cayenne, optional

Rinse beans and soak for several hours or overnight. Pour off soaking water, add fresh water to cover beans, and bring to boil. Reduce heat to low, cover, and cook about 1 $^1/_2$ to 2 hours until tender. Add water as necessary to just cover beans. Set beans aside.

Heat oil at medium heat in a gallon saucepan. Add onions and garlic, stir briefly, then add green pepper. Sauté until onions are translucent. Add mild chili powder, cumin, and pepper. Stir briefly. Add the tomatoes including liquid. Pour in cooked beans including liquid. Add water, salt, brown sugar, and cayenne. Cook covered for 30 to 40 minutes on low heat. Stir occasionally.

Nutritional Analysis (per serving)

Calories 230	Carbohydrates .... 32.8 g
Calories from fat 30%	Dietary fiber .... 10.4 g
Total fat .... 8.03 g	Cholesterol .... 0 mg
Protein.. .... 9.69 g	Sodium .... 501 mg

Chicken Quinoa Salad

(pronounced "Keenwa")

MARY DE ROSAS, SEATTLE

Serves 6

1 cup quinoa, rinsed (a high-protein grain)
1 pound chicken breasts, skinned and boned
juice of 2 limes
3 tablespoons olive oil
$^1/_3$ cup fresh cilantro, chopped
1 cucumber, peeled, seeded and chopped
3 tomatoes, chopped
2 $^1/_2$-ounce sliced black olives
crushed red pepper
limes, optional

Cube chicken breast and place in marinade of lime juice and olive oil.

Marinate in refrigerator for several hours.

Place quinoa with 2 cups of water in a saucepan and bring to boil. Reduce to simmer, cover and cook until all water is absorbed, about 15 minutes. Quinoa is done when grains have turned from white to transparent and the spiral-like germ is separated.

Sauté chicken in 1 tablespoon of marinade, reserving the remainder. When chicken has cooked thoroughly, add to quinoa. Add reserved marinade, cilantro, cucumber, tomato, and olives. Mix well.

Garnish with additional limes, and/or lime juice and crushed red pepper if preferred. Serve warm or chilled on a bed of lettuce.

Nutritional Analysis (per serving)

Calories 224	Carbohydrates .... 12.8 g
Calories from fat 42%	Dietary fiber .... 3.69 g
Total fat .... 10.7 g	Cholesterol .... 43.6 mg
Protein.. .... 20.0 g	Sodium .... 145 mg

Dale's Magnificent Muffins

KATHLEEN KLEIN, SEATTLE

Makes 24 medium-sized muffins

3 cups bran
2 $^1/_3$ cups skim milk
$^1/_3$ cup brown sugar
$^2/_3$ cup molasses
juice of one orange
rind of orange, chopped fine
$^2/_3$ cup walnuts
1 cup raisins
1 shredded carrot
$^1/_3$ cup vegetable oil
2 eggs, beaten
1 teaspoon anise seed
3 cups whole wheat flour
1 teaspoon baking soda
4 teaspoons baking powder

In a very large mixing bowl, combine bran, milk, brown sugar, molasses, juice and rind of orange, walnuts, raisins, carrot, vegetable oil, eggs, and anise seed. In a second bowl, combine flour, baking soda, and baking powder.

Stir dry ingredients into wet ingredients until just blended. If mixture is too runny, add a little flour. If too dry, add skim milk.

Spoon the mixture into lightly greased muffin tins, filling halfway. Bake for 25 to 30 minutes at 350 degrees. Cool for 10 to 15 minutes before removing from tin.

Nutritional Analysis (per serving)

Calories 177	Carbohydrates .... 29.6 g
Calories from fat 38%	Dietary fiber .... 4.61 g
Total fat .... 6.07 g	Cholesterol .... 17.7 mg
Protein.. .... 4.85 g	Sodium .... 58.3 mg

Dill Cottage Cheese Bread

ANN SCHMIDT, SEATTLE

Makes 1 loaf

¹/₄ cup warm water
1 teaspoon honey
1 tablespoon yeast
1 cup low fat cottage cheese
1 egg
1 tablespoon honey
¹/₂ teaspoon salt
2 teaspoons dill weed
1 teaspoon dill seed
2 tablespoons onion, finely chopped
¹/₄ teaspoon soda
2 tablespoons oil
2 ¹/₂ to 3 cups flour

Mix warm water, honey, and yeast, and set aside. Heat cottage cheese until warm, being careful not to boil. Add egg, honey, salt, dill weed and seed, onion, soda, and oil to cottage cheese. Stir in yeast mixture. Beat in 1 cup flour for 5 minutes. Stir in the rest of flour. Do not knead. Cover, let rise for 1 hour. Punch down. Put in a greased loaf pan and let rise for about 30 minutes, or until double. Bake for 45 to 50 minutes at 350 degrees.

Nutritional Analysis (per serving)

Calories 154	Carbohydrates .... 24.5 g
Calories from fat 19%	Dietary fiber .... 1.02 g
Total fat .... 3.20 g	Cholesterol .... 18.2 mg
Protein.. .... 6.16 g	Sodium .... 190 mg

Eggplant Lasagna

NANCY N. SOREIDE, SEATTLE

Serves 4 to 6

1 medium eggplant
1 to 2 tablespoons olive oil
8 large mushrooms
12-ounce lasagna noodles
³/₄ cup grated mozzarella cheese
12-ounces low fat ricotta cheese

Tomato Sauce

1 28-ounce can tomatoes, chopped
1 tablespoon tomato paste
1 large onion, chopped
2 tablespoons olive oil
1 to 4 garlic cloves
1 teaspoon dried hot red pepper flakes
2 teaspoons dried basil
2 teaspoons dried oregano
1 teaspoon dried thyme
grated black pepper, to taste

Sauté onion in olive oil until transparent. Add all the other sauce ingredients and let the sauce simmer on medium-low heat.

Slice the eggplant crosswise into ¹/₄-inch to ¹/₂-inch slices. Do not peel the eggplant. Brush the slices with olive oil on both sides and place on a baking sheet about 10 inches below the broiler. Broil until they are softened, turning once. This takes 5 to 6 minutes on each side. Slice the mushrooms into thick (¹/₄-¹/₂") slices. Cook lasagne noodles according to package directions. Drain.

Layer the ingredients in a 9-x-13-inch pan. Start with a small amount of sauce in the bottom, followed by a layer of noodles. Add a layer of eggplant and mushroom slices. Dot with ricotta cheese and sprinkle with mozzarella. Top with sauce. Continue to layer the ingredients, ending with a layer of noodles topped with sauce.

Cover with aluminum foil or a lid and bake at 350 degrees for 1 hour and 15 minutes.

Nutritional Analysis (per serving)

Calories 401	Carbohydrates .... 50.0 g
Calories from fat 30%	Dietary fiber .... 8.88 g
Total fat .... 13.7 g	Cholesterol .... 68.9 mg
Protein.. .... 21.9 g	Sodium .... 412 mg

Health Bread

BEVERLY K. ULLIN, SEATTLE

Makes 24 servings

2 cups whole wheat flour
2 cups unbleached flour
1 cup cornmeal
1 cup oat bran
1 cup wheat bran
1/2 teaspoon salt
1 cup molasses
4 teaspoons baking soda
1 quart buttermilk
1 cup raisins
1 cup chopped walnuts
1 cup chopped dates, prunes, or
*   additional raisins*

In a large bowl, mix flour, cornmeal, oat bran, wheat bran, and salt. Add molasses. Rinse molasses cup with ⅓ cup hot tap water and add to mix with baking soda. Add buttermilk and stir well. Add raisins, walnuts, and your choice of dates, prunes, or additional raisins. Pour batter into greased bread pans. For two large loaves, bake 1 hour 25 minutes at 325 degrees. For four

small loaves, bake 1 hour 15 minutes at 325 degrees.

Nutritional Analysis (per serving)

Calories 222	Carbohydrates .... 44.2 g
Calories from fat 16%	Dietary fiber .... 4.54 g
Total fat .... 4.12 g	Cholesterol .... 1.50 mg
Protein.. .... 6.26 g	Sodium .... 229 mg

Italian Tabouli

P. SOTTILE, TACOMA

Serves 6

2 cups bulghur wheat
3 cups water
1/2 red onion, finely chopped
1 medium cucumber, finely chopped
1 large tomato, cut in small chunks
1/2 cup vinegar
3 teaspoons dried parsley
1 teaspoon oregano
1 teaspoon basil

Bring water to boil. Pour boiling water into a bowl over bulghur. Cover with a dish towel and let soak 45 minutes until water is absorbed. Add onion, cucumber, and tomato to the bulgur mixture. Add vinegar and spices. Mix gently. Cover and chill for about 3 hours before serving. Excellent as a salad, or as lunch in pocket bread. Keeps well in refrigerator.

Nutritional Analysis (per serving)

Calories 212	Carbohydrates .... 46.4 g
Calories from fat 4%	Dietary fiber .... 11.0 g
Total fat .... 0.950 g	Cholesterol .... 0 mg
Protein.. .... 6.75 g	Sodium .... 8.31 mg

Herb Onion Whole Wheat Rolls

JUDY RAINWATER, KIRKLAND

Serves 24

1/4 cup warm water
2 packages dry active yeast (2 tablespoons)

1 ³/₄ cup warm water (may substitute milk and eliminate powdered dry milk)
1 tablespoon margarine
2 tablespoons sugar
¹/₂ cup powdered non fat dry milk
¹/₄ cup chopped onion
1 tablespoon dill weed (may substitute 1 tablespoon basil or 1 tablespoon Italian seasoning)
2 tablespoons salt
2 cups whole wheat flour
2 to 4 cups bread flour

Mix ¹/₄ cup warm water, yeast and 1 teaspoon sugar in a small bowl. Let stand until dissolved. In mixing bowl mix 1 ³/₄ cup warm water, margarine, sugar, powdered milk, onion, dill weed, salt, and 2 cups whole wheat flour. Beat well. Add yeast mixture and beat well. Add remaining flour until dough is stiff. Turn dough out onto a lightly floured board and knead for 5 minutes or until smooth and elastic. Cover, let rise for 45 minutes or until double.

When dough is ready, punch it down and divide into rolls. Place on lightly greased baking sheet. Let rise for 30 minutes or until double in size. Bake for 25 to 30 minutes at 350 degrees.

Nutritional Analysis (per serving)

Calories	90.0	Carbohydrates	18.7 g
Calories from fat	6%	Dietary fiber	1.73 g
Total fat	0.574 g	Cholesterol	0.250 mg
Protein..	2 .86 g	Sodium	548 mg

Lentils & Rice Casserole

Jeni St. Claire, Spokane

Serves 6

2 ²/₃ cups chicken broth
³/₄ cup dry lentils
¹/₂ cup brown rice
³/₄ cup chopped onion
¹/₂ cup chopped or grated carrot (optional)
¹/₄ teaspoon oregano

¹/₄ teaspoon thyme
¹/₄ teaspoon garlic salt or powder
¹/₂ teaspoon crushed basil
4 ounces Monterey Jack cheese or cheddar cheese, grated

Mix all ingredients together. Bake in 1 ¹/₂-quart casserole (lightly greased) for 1 ¹/₂ hours at 350 degrees or until lentils are done.

Note: Other vegetables such as mushrooms or celery may be added.

Nutritional Analysis (per serving)

Calories	244	Carbohydrates	30.6 g
Calories from fat	26%	Dietary fiber	5.24 g
Total fat	6.98 g	Cholesterol	17.7 mg
Protein	15.1 g	Sodium	450 mg

Lentil Salad

S.M. Estvanik, Seattle

Serves 4

1 ¹/₂ cup lentils
1 medium onion, sliced thin
1 red pepper, cut julienne
1 small hot pepper, sliced
¹/₄ cup parsley, chopped
2 tablespoons olive oil
1 tablespoon vinegar
3 tablespoons parsley

Cook lentils following instructions on package, but undercook slightly. Cool, then add onion, peppers, and seasonings. Mix quickly, then chill before serving.

Nutritional Analysis (per serving)

Calories	325	Carbohydrates	46.2 g
Calories from fat	20%	Dietary fiber	9.99 g
Total fat	7.67 g	Cholesterol	0 mg
Protein..	21.1 g	Sodium	12.0 mg

Lunchtime Bean Spread

CHRISTINE BONFILIO, HOODSPORT

Serves 6

1 cup cooked beans, any combination of
   black, red, white or garbanzo beans
$^1/_4$ cup chopped celery
$^1/_4$ cup chopped onion
1 tablespoon nonfat plain yogurt
1 tablespoon lemon juice
$^1/_8$ teaspoon salt
$^1/_8$ teaspoon garlic powder
dash pepper
1 teaspoon crushed oregano
6 slices whole wheat bread
6 slices of onion, optional
tomato slices
3 ounces thinly sliced Monterey Jack cheese

Mash cooked beans with fork, or put
through food mill. Add celery, onion,
yogurt, lemon juice, salt, garlic powder,
pepper, and oregano. Mix with fork.
Toast bread slices. Spread bean mixture
evenly on each slice of bread. Top with
onion slices, if used, tomato, and cheese.

Broil until cheese melts and bubbles
slightly. Makes 6 open-faced
sandwiches.

Nutritional Analysis (per serving)

Calories	172	Carbohydrates	21.7 g
Calories from fat	30%	Dietary fiber	3.77 g
Total fat	5.91 g	Cholesterol	13.0 mg
Protein..	8.77 g	Sodium	279 mg

Maple Oat Bran Muffins

NANCY DOUGLAS, PORT ORCHARD

Serves 15

5 teaspoons ground cinnamon
$^1/_4$ teaspoon ground nutmeg
$^1/_2$ teaspoon salt
2 teaspoons baking powder
2 $^1/_4$ cups oat bran
$^1/_2$ cup sugar or honey
1 grated apple
$^1/_2$ cup egg substitute, or $^1/_2$ cup egg
   whites with $^1/_4$ teaspoon oil
1 cup low fat milk or fruit juice
1 teaspoon vanilla
1 teaspoon maple extract
2 teaspoons oil
$^1/_2$ cup raisins
$^1/_2$ cup sliced almonds, optional

Line 15 muffin cups with paper liners.
In small bowl combine raisins with $^1/_4$
cup milk or juice. Heat in microwave
until hot. Set aside. In a large bowl, mix
all dry ingredients thoroughly. In a
separate bowl, mix remaining
ingredients. Stir into dry ingredients.
Add raisins and mix.

Fill paper liners in muffin cups. Bake for
20 minutes at 425 degrees.

Nutritional Analysis (per serving)

Calories	117	Carbohydrates	24.8 g
Calories from fat	20%	Dietary fiber	3.51 g
Total fat	3.20 g	Cholesterol	0.667 mg
Protein..	4.15 g	Sodium	197 mg

Meatless Lasagna

AIMEE HESKETH, SEATTLE

Serves 8

1 box lasagna noodles
1 to 2 tablespoons oil
2 to 3 medium zucchini, sliced $^1/_4$-inch thick
2 cups mozzarella cheese, shredded
$^1/_4$ to $^1/_2$ cup Parmesan cheese
1 28-ounce can tomatoes, chopped
2 small or 1 large can tomato paste
1 $^1/_2$ cup water
1 pound cottage cheese
2 cloves garlic, chopped
1 tablespoon butter
$^1/_2$ teaspoon basil
$^1/_2$ teaspoon Italian seasoning
2 teaspoons dried onion flakes

Sauté garlic in 1 tablespoon butter. Add
canned tomatoes, tomato paste, water,

and seasonings. Stir and let simmer on low for approximately 10 minutes. Add cottage cheese and slowly stir until blended. Set aside.

Cook noodles in boiling water. Add 1 to 2 tablespoons oil to keep noodles from sticking together. Drain and set aside.

To assemble, start with sauce on bottom of dish. Add layer of zucchini, then mozzarella cheese, then noodles. Repeat layering, ending with sauce and mozzarella cheese. Top everything with Parmesan cheese. Bake for 45 to 50 minutes at 350 degrees.

Nutritional Analysis (per serving)

Calories	267	Carbohydrates	29.8 g
Calories from fat	30%	Dietary fiber	4.76 g
Total fat	9.08 g	Cholesterol	42.0 mg
Protein..	18.2 g	Sodium	592 mg

Mixed Fruit & Whole Wheat Tea Bread

DIANA FITSCHEN, PUYALLUP

Makes 16 slices

3 cups whole wheat flour
3 teaspoons baking powder
$^1/_2$ teaspoon salt
1 teaspoon ground cinnamon
$^1/_4$ teaspoon ground mace
$^1/_4$ teaspoon ground nutmeg
$^1/_4$ teaspoon ground ginger
1 large egg, beaten
1 $^1/_4$ cups nonfat milk
1 cup honey
2 tablespoons salad oil
1 cup dried mixed fruits, chopped
1 cup walnuts, chopped
grated rind of lemon

Stir together flour, baking powder, salt, cinnamon, mace, nutmeg, and ginger. In a small bowl, blend egg, milk, honey, and oil. Pour over flour mixture and stir just enough to moisten. Fold in mixed fruits, walnuts, and grated lemon rind.

Turn into greased 9-x-5-x-3-inch bread pan.

Bake for 60 to 70 minutes at 350 degrees. Cake tester inserted in center should come out clean. Let stand 10 minutes. Loosen edges and turn out on wire rack, then turn right-side up. Cool completely. Cut into 16 thin slices.

Nutritional Analysis (per serving)

Calories	245	Carbohydrates	42.9 g
Calories from fat	25%	Dietary fiber	1.44 g
Total fat	6.99 g	Cholesterol	13.3 mg
Protein..	4.84 g	Sodium	84.3 mg

Pasta Salad Primavera

DIANA STANTON, SPOKANE

Serves 8

1 cup green split peas, rinsed and drained
4 cups water
$^1/_4$ cup white wine vinegar
1 garlic clove, minced
1 tablespoon dijon mustard
$^1/_4$ teaspoon crushed red pepper flakes
$^1/_2$ teaspoon salt
$^1/_4$ teaspoon pepper
$^1/_4$ cup salad oil
2 tablespoons olive oil
4 cups cooked small pasta
1 $^1/_2$ cup diced red or green pepper
1 $^1/_2$ cup thinly sliced green onion

In sauce pan, combine peas and water. Cover and bring to boil. Reduce heat. Simmer for 10 minutes or until peas are just tender. Meanwhile, combine vinegar, garlic, mustard, red pepper, salt and pepper. Beat in oils. Add pasta, peas and remaining ingredients. Toss and chill.

Nutritional Analysis (per serving)

Calories	245	Carbohydrates	30.1 g
Calories from fat	39%	Dietary fiber	5.11 g
Total fat	10.8 g	Cholesterol	0 mg
Protein..	8.55 g	Sodium	118 mg

Pasta with Red Lentil Sauce

Thomas Iberle, Seattle

Serves 6

2 tablespoons margarine
2 tablespoons olive oil
1 cup onion, chopped
3 to 4 cloves garlic, minced
2 teaspoons basil
1 teaspoon oregano
salt and pepper to taste
2 15-ounce cans tomato sauce
$^1/_2$ pound fresh mushrooms, chopped
1 to 2 tablespoons red wine (optional)
$^2/_3$ cup lentils
1 pound pasta (mostaccioli or wagon
    wheels recommended)

Put lentils in a saucepan and cover with water. Bring to a boil and simmer 20 to 25 minutes. Drain and set aside.

Sauté onions and garlic in margarine and olive oil with basil, oregano, salt and pepper until soft, 3 to 5 minutes. Add tomato sauce, mushrooms, and wine. Simmer at least 20 to 30 minutes.

Add cooked lentils 5 to 10 minutes before serving and stir. Continue simmering. Pour sauce over cooked, drained pasta and serve.

Nutritional Analysis (per serving)

Calories 366	Carbohydrates .... 62.8 g
Calories from fat 18%	Dietary fiber .... 8.69 g
Total fat .... 7.80 g	Cholesterol .... 0 mg
Protein.. .... 14.6 g	Sodium .... 997 mg

Pasta Vesuvius Style

Evelyn V. Mineo, Bellevue

Serves 4

$^3/_4$ pound fusilli (twisted noodles)
$^1/_2$ pound ripe tomatoes
$^1/_4$ cup olive oil
1 teaspoon minced fresh basil
    (or $^1/_2$ teaspoon dried)

1 teaspoon minced oregano
$^1/_2$ cup diced low fat mozzarella cheese
$^1/_4$ cup Parmesan cheese
2 grindings of fresh black pepper

Chop unpeeled tomatoes, squeeze out some of the seeds and discard them. Heat olive oil in wide pan Add chopped tomatoes and herbs. Cook for 15 minutes, stirring occasionally.

Meanwhile cook noodles al dente (just until tender). Drain thoroughly. Stir in tomato sauce, mozzarella and Parmesan. Heat together until cheeses have melted. Sprinkle with freshly ground pepper and serve immediately.

Nutritional Analysis (per serving)

Calories 355	Carbohydrates .... 42.6 g
Calories from fat 35%	Dietary fiber .... 3.13 g
Total fat .... 13.8 g	Cholesterol .... 19.9 mg
Protein.. .... 15.7 g	Sodium .... 233 mg

Pumpkin & Raisin Muffins

Jill Silver, Seattle

Makes 15 medium-sized muffins

2 cups whole wheat flour, regular or pastry
1 teaspoon baking soda
$^1/_2$ teaspoon salt
1 teaspoon cinnamon
$^1/_2$ teaspoon nutmeg
$^1/_2$ cup rolled oats or oat flour, optional
1 egg, optional
$^1/_3$ cup safflower oil
$^1/_3$ cup unsulphured molasses
$^1/_2$ cup brown sugar
$^2/_3$ cup nonfat milk, buttermilk or
    nonfat yogurt
1 cup mashed pumpkin
$^3/_4$ cup raisins

In a small bowl, combine and stir flour, baking soda, salt, cinnamon, nutmeg, and, if desired, rolled oats or oat flour. In a large bowl, combine egg, safflower oil, molasses, brown sugar, milk or yogurt, pumpkin, and raisins.

Mix the dry ingredients with the wet, stirring until just blended. Spoon into prepared muffin tins. Bake for 15 to 20 minutes at 400 degrees.

Nutritional Analysis (per serving)

Calories 194	Carbohydrates .... 34.7 g
Calories from fat 24%	Dietary fiber .... 3.62 g
Total fat .... 5.37 g	Cholesterol .... 14.0 mg
Protein.. .... 4.31 g	Sodium .... 142 mg

Rice & Leeks

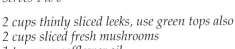

Christine Bonfilio, Hoodsport

Serves 4 to 6

2 cups thinly sliced leeks, use green tops also
2 cups sliced fresh mushrooms
1 teaspoon safflower oil
2 cups cooked brown rice
¹/₄ teaspoon crushed marjoram
¹/₈ teaspoon salt
dash pepper

Wash leeks thoroughly and slice crosswise. Sauté leeks and mushrooms in oil over, using a large skillet over medium heat. Stir frequently and cook until mushrooms appear done and leeks still a bit crispy. Add marjoram, salt and pepper. Stir in cooked brown rice and heat thoroughly.

Nutritional Analysis (per serving)

Calories 111	Carbohydrates .... 22.6 g
Calories from fat 11%	Dietary fiber .... 2.37 g
Total fat .... 1.35 g	Cholesterol .... 0 mg
Protein.. .... 2.65 g	Sodium .... 52.4 mg

Spanish Rice

Molly McLaughlin, Bellingham

Serves 6

1 ¹/₂ cup brown rice
¹/₄ cup oil
2 cloves garlic, slivered

¹/₃ cup chopped onion
¹/₃ cup sunflower seeds
¹/₃ cup chopped green pepper
2 cups chopped tomatoes
1 ³/₄ cups water
dash hot pepper sauce
1 teaspoon paprika
salt to taste

Wash rice and drain well. Heat oil in large pot and medium heat. Add garlic, onion and sunflower seeds and stir about 3 minutes. Add rice and green pepper and stir a few more minutes. Add remaining ingredients. Bring to boil, reduce heat and simmer, covered, for about an hour. Stir as needed to prevent sticking.

Nutritional Analysis (per serving)

Calories 260	Carbohydrates .... 30.4 g
Calories from fat 47%	Dietary fibr .... 3.42 g
Total fat .... 13.8 g	Cholesterol .... 0 mg
Protein.. .... 5.05 g	Sodium .... 5.91 mg

Spinach & Water Chestnut Bread Dip

Jan Bogle, Seattle

Serves 12

1 large round loaf sourdough or whole wheat bread
1 box frozen chopped spinach, thawed
1 can water chestnuts, chopped
1 cup low fat plain yogurt
1 cup imitation mayonnaise
onion powder to taste

Mix thawed spinach, water chestnuts, onion powder, yogurt, and mayonnaise in medium bowl. Refrigerate one day to allow flavors to blend.

To serve, hollow out loaf of bread; make 1-inch chunks of bread from hollowed bread. Fill hollowed loaf with dip. Arrange round loaf and bread cubes on tray. Bread cubes may be dipped. Use of dill casserole bread provides an interesting and delicious variation.

Nutritional Analysis (per serving)

Calories 186	Carbohydrates .... 27.9 g
Calories from fat 29%	Dietary fiber .... 4.34 g
Total fat .... 6.37 g	Cholesterol .... 6.50 mg
Protein.. .... 6.54 g	Sodium .... 434 mg

Summary Pasta Salad

JULIE NIERENBERG, ISSAQUAH

Serves 6

Lowfat Yogurt Dressing

¹/₂ cup low fat plain yogurt
¹/₄ cup grated Parmesan cheese
¹/₂ cup low fat cottage cheese
1 tablespoon lemon juice
2 teaspoons dried dill weed
black pepper and garlic powder to taste

Pasta Salad

1 cup celery, chopped
1 cup tomato, diced
1 cup green pepper, diced
¹/₄ cup onion, chopped
1 ¹/₂ cups chicken, tuna, or ham, diced
1 ¹/₂ cups colored corkscrew macaroni,
*   cooked & cooled*
¹/₂ teaspoon salt

Blend all dressing ingredients, using puree setting.

Mix salad ingredients together. Add lowfat yogurt dressing. Mix again. Serve on crisp lettuce leaves.

Nutritional Analysis (per serving)

Calories 187	Carbohydrates .... 18.0 g
Calories from fat 24%	Dietary fiber .... 1.89 g
Total fat .... 5.06 g	Cholesterol .... 37.6 mg
Protein.. .... 17.3 g	Sodium .... 377 mg

Three Grain Waffles

FRANCES B. NORSTRAND, SEATTLE

Makes 10 half-waffle servings

1 cup whole wheat flour
¹/₂ cup yellow corn meal

¹/₂ cup soy flour
1 teaspoon double-acting baking powder
¹/₂ teaspoon baking soda
¹/₄ to ¹/₂ teaspoon salt, optional
2 ¹/₄ cups nonfat buttermilk
¹/₄ cup corn or safflower oil, or melted
*   margarine*
2 large eggs

In a large bowl, mix flours, corn meal, baking powder, soda, and salt. In another bowl, beat eggs, add buttermilk, and mix well. Add dry ingredients and mix well. Add oil.

Let stand from 3 to 5 minutes, to thicken. You may need to thin the batter with some more buttermilk until it is the right consistency. Bake on greased waffle iron. Serve with your favorite syrup or jam. These waffles freeze well.

Nutritional Analysis (per serving)

Calories 169	Carbohydrates .... 18.5 g
Calories from fat 43%	Dietary fiber .... 2.62 g
Total fat .... 7.58 g	Cholesterol .... 43.6 mg
Protein.. .... 7.80 g	Sodium .... 145 mg

Whole Wheat Pancakes

DAVID BITTENBENDER, SEATTLE

Makes 6 2-pancake servings

1 ¹/₂ cups stone ground whole wheat flour
2 ¹/₂ teaspoons baking powder
2 egg whites
1 ¹/₂ to 2 cups nonfat, fortified milk
1 to 2 tablespoons honey, optional
1 to 2 bananas, mashed, optional
1 apples, chopped or grated, optional
1 cup blueberries, optional
1 cup crushed pineapple, optional
1 teaspoon safflower oil

Heat cast iron skillet or equivalent on stove. Grease lightly with safflower oil. Mix together flour and baking powder. Add egg whites, and milk. Stir. If desired, add any of the optional

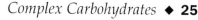

ingredients and stir in. Cook in skillet until brown. Top with yogurt, low sugar jelly, or low sugar syrup.

Nutritional Analysis (per serving)

Calories 147	Carbohydrates .... 28.7 g
Calories from fat 4%	Dietary fiber .... 3.77 g
Total fat .... 0.747 g	Cholesterol .... 1.33 mg
Protein.. .... 7.91 g	Sodium .... 190 mg

Wild-Rice Stuffed Acorn Squash

LISA MAYNARD, SEATTLE

Serves 6

2 tablespoons safflower oil
1 small onion, chopped
1 clove garlic, crushed
1/4 pound mushrooms, chopped, optional
1 teaspoon dried thyme
1/2 cup wild rice
1 cup brown rice

3 cups hot water or vegetable broth
3 acorn squash, halved with seeds removed
tamari, to taste

Sauté onions, garlic and mushrooms until soft. Add rice. Sauté 4 to 5 minutes until starting to brown. Add water or broth and bring to boil. Reduce heat. Cover and cook for 40 minutes or until water is absorbed. Add pepper, thyme and tamari to taste.

Meanwhile, lightly oil cut edge of squash. Turn upside down on baking sheet. Bake at 300 degrees until soft to fork.

Mound rice mixture in squash shells. Return to oven for several minutes to heat through.

Nutritional Analysis (per serving)

Calories 278	Carbohydrates .... 53.4 g
Calories from fat 18%	Dietary fiber .... 5.16 g
Total fat .... 5.72 g	Cholesterol .... 0 mg
Protein.. .... 5.36 g	Sodium .... 67.2 mg

Poultry & Seafood

▲▲▲▲▲▲▲▲▲▲▲▲▲▲▲▲▲

Poultry & Seafood

I f you're interested in good nutrition, you can't have too many recipes for healthy ways to cook poultry and seafood. Advice from medical and nutrition experts is unanimous: Cut down on fat in your diet by eating more chicken, turkey, and seafood, and less red meat.

Whether you bake, roast, barbecue, broil, stew, boil, poach, or steam it, chicken is a smart choice for people trying to limit fat in their diets—and that should be just about everybody. A three-ounce serving of baked, skinless chicken has just 116 calories and less than two grams of fat. But remember to remove the skin—that's where most of the fat in the chicken is located. And make fried chicken a special-occasion splurge rather than part of the weekly rotation.

Be aware that when you order chicken at most fast-food restaurants, you're getting a product that has as much or more fat than most beef items because it often has been deep-fried in oil.

Try these tips for preparing poultry:

◆ Remove skin and fat before eating poultry. If you remove the skin and fat before cooking, you avoid fat that drips into the meat.

◆ Roast poultry on a rack so it does not sit in the fatty drippings.

◆ Don't baste with drippings. Fruit juice or white wine make good basting ingredients.

◆ Before making gravy, refrigerate the drippings so the fat can congeal and be skimmed off. Bring de-fatted drippings to a boil, add a mixture of flour and water and stir briskly.

◆ Bake dressing in a separate casserole dish and not inside the bird.

◆ Microwaving is a quick and easy way to cook chicken breasts.

◆ Poultry is finished cooking when a fork can be inserted easily and the juices run clear.

◆ Cook poultry immediately after thawing to minimize the risk of food-born illness such as Salmonella.

◆ Stir-fry bite-sized pieces of poultry with fresh vegetables and serve over rice for a fast-food meal that beats what the chains have to offer.

▲▲▲▲▲▲▲▲▲▲▲▲▲▲▲▲▲▲

For good nutrition, seafood is an excellent choice and should be included in your diet at least three times a week, according to nutritionists. Fish is a protein source with some cholesterol, but very little fat—and most of the fat is unsaturated.

Even shellfish, which at one time was thought to be too high in cholesterol, is now considered an excellent choice because its saturated fat content is low.

A three-ounce serving of halibut has 116 calories. Monkfish has 80 and sole has 100 calories per three ounces. Crab has about 90 calories per serving, clams have 126, and mussels top the list at 147 per three ounces.

When cooking fish, experts recommend following the 10-minute rule: Cook the fish or fish fillet 10 minutes per inch of thickness. Fish is done when it flakes easily with a fork and when the flesh is opaque.

If you are microwaving fish, allow about three minutes per pound at high power. Remove from the microwave oven when the center is still translucent but the outer edges are opaque, because the center will continue to cook a bit on its own.

Always defrost frozen fish in its original wrapping and cook within two days of defrosting.

If you purchase canned fish such as tuna or salmon, buy varieties that have been packed in water or fish oil, not vegetable oil. If you rinse the canned fish in water, you can reduce the sodium content by half—not a bad idea, considering that canned products are always fairly high in sodium.

Recommended portion sizes of both poultry and seafood are three to four ounces per serving—about the size of a deck of playing cards.

Poultry and seafood are both excellently suited for adding to salads—either vegetable salads or pasta salads or any combination of pasta and vegetables. Add a little low-calorie salad dressing or make a dressing out of yogurt and seasonings and you have an all-in-one-dish meal.

On the following pages you'll find new recipes to add to your repertoire of tasty, low fat main dishes, soups, and appetizers.

Baked Snapper with Dressing

BOB HEFFERNAN, SEATTLE

Serves 6

$^1/_2$ *cup chopped onions*
$^1/_2$ *cup chopped celery*
$^1/_2$ *cup fresh mushrooms*
2 pounds snapper filet
2 tablespoons margarine
2 cups soft bread crumbs
$^1/_4$ *teaspoon salt*
$^1/_4$ *teaspoon pepper*
pinch of dried tarragon or rosemary
lemon juice
3 to 4 tomatoes

Sauté onions, celery, and mushrooms in margarine for 5 minutes. Stir in bread crumbs, salt, pepper, tarragon, and rosemary. Put snapper in baking dish. Sprinkle with lemon juice. Spread dressing on snapper. Slice tomatoes and place on top. Bake uncovered for 35 to 40 minutes at 375 degrees.

Nutritional Analysis (per serving)

Calories	235	Carbohydrates	12.1 g
Calories from fat	19%	Dietary fiber	1.71 g
Total fat	4.75 g	Cholesterol	57.7 mg
Protein..	34.5 g	Sodium	385 mg

Calamari Bangkok

S.M. ESTVANIK, SEATTLE

Serves 4

*2 pounds squid, cleaned and
    cut into rings*
4 tablespoons fresh basil, chopped
*1 small green Thai chili, or jalapeño,
    chopped*
1 pound broccoli, cut into small pieces
1 small onion, sliced
1 $^1/_2$ tablespoons peanut oil

Stir-fry onion and broccoli in hot peanut oil. Add squid and cook quickly. Toss in basil and chili, then reduce heat. Serve with rice.

Nutritional Analysis (per serving)

Calories	278	Carbohydrates	14.6 g
Calories from fat	26%	Dietary fiber	4.68 g
Total fat	7.99 g	Cholesterol	109 mg
Protein	37.9 g	Sodium	63.5 mg

Chicken Cordon Verde

SELMA COLE, BOTHELL

Serves 4

*2 chicken breasts, skinned, boned, and
    halved*
*4 canned green chilies, cut open, seeds
    removed*
4 thin slices jack cheese ($^3/_4$ ounce each)
2 tablespoons flour
$^1/_4$ *teaspoon nutmeg*
2 tablespoons safflower oil
$^3/_4$ *cup prepared green chili salsa*
$^1/_4$ *cup sliced almonds*
4 sprigs fresh cilantro
1 tomato, cut in thin wedges

Place chicken between two sheets of waxed paper. Pound with a rubber mallet or rolling pin until thin. Put one green chili on each piece of chicken, then a slice of cheese over the green chile. Roll up, tucking in ends, and secure with wooden tooth picks. Dust each roll with flour and sprinkle with nutmeg.

Heat safflower oil in a non-stick skillet. Brown chicken rolls on all sides at medium heat. Cover. Reduce heat to low. Cook 5 to 8 minutes more. Chicken juices should run clear when pierced with a fork, and cheese should be melted.

While chicken rolls are cooking, heat green chili salsa in a small sauce pan.

Reduce liquid to a medium thick sauce. Add sliced almonds to sauce. Transfer chicken rolls to a warmed platter. Pour some of the sauce over each roll and garnish with cilantro sprigs and tomato wedges.

Nutritional Analysis (per serving)

Calories 333	Carbohydrates .... 16.6 g
Calories from fat 54%	Dietary fiber .... 4.34 g
Total fat .... 20.5 g	Cholesterol .... 56.0 mg
Protein.. .... 22.5 g	Sodium .... 211 mg

Chicken Lime Soup

CAROLE MERIAM, VASHON ISLAND

Serves 6

4 cups chicken broth
2 chicken breast halves skinned
$^1/_3$ cup alphabet pasta
$^1/_3$ cup chopped red onion
$^1/_4$ cup fresh lime juice (1 to 2 limes)
$^1/_4$ cup chopped fresh cilantro
1 small ripe avocado, peeled, pitted and sliced

In saucepan, bring broth to a boil. Add chicken, reduce to simmer, cover and cook 20 minutes. Remove chicken from broth. Cool slightly, then pull meat off the bones and shred. Set aside.

Reheat broth to boiling. Add pasta, reduce heat to low boil, cover, and cook for 10 minutes. Add onion, lime juice, chicken, cilantro, and avocado. Cover and simmer for 5 minutes.

Nutritional Analysis (per serving)

Calories 151	Carbohydrates .... 8.19 g
Calories from fat 42%	Dietary fiber .... 3.60 g
Total fat .... 7.12 g	Cholesterol .... 25.0 mg
Protein.. .... 13.8 g	Sodium .... 541 mg

Chicken Olé

ERIN OTIS, BELLINGHAM

Serves 4

1 cup cooked and diced chicken meat (skinless)
1 4-ounce can chopped green chilies
1 8-ounce carton plain nonfat yogurt
$^1/_2$ cup lowfat grated cheese
$^1/_2$ cup sliced fresh mushrooms
$^1/_4$ cup chopped green pepper
$^1/_4$ cup chopped green onion
2 cups unsalted blue corn tortilla chips

Mix all ingredients together (except chips). Set aside. Line 8-inch square casserole dish with half of the chips then pour half of the chicken mixture on top. Add remainder of chips over that and finally pour last half of the chicken mixture on top. Bake for 45 minutes at 350 degrees or microwave on high for 15 to 20 minutes.

Nutritional Analysis (per serving)

Calories 383	Carbohydrates .... 41.7 g
Calories from fat 39%	Dietary fiber .... 3.06 g
Total fat .... 17.2 g	Cholesterol .... 26.0 mg
Protein.. .... 17.6 g	Sodium .... 362 mg

Chicken Teppan-Sari

CARRIE MARGOLIN, TACOMA

Serves 6

1 cut-up fryer chicken, 3 to 4 pounds
$^1/_4$ cup white wine or sherry
$^1/_8$ cup worcestershire sauce
$^1/_8$ cup low sodium soy sauce
$^1/_4$ cup water
2 teaspoons parsley flakes
2 teaspoons toasted sesame seeds
2 teaspoons oregano
1 teaspoon granulated garlic powder
1 teaspoon curry powder
1 teaspoon basil
$^1/_2$ teaspoon celery seed

Remove all skin and fat from chicken. Separate thighs from drumsticks.

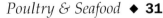

Arrange the chicken pieces, single layer, in a microwave-safe casserole. Sprinkle with wine, worcestershire, and soy. Add water to the liquids in the casserole to double the liquids but don't pour water over the chicken.

Sprinkle chicken with half of each of the dry spices. The amount of each spice should be enough to create a light but complete covering on the chicken (for a large chicken, increase the spices accordingly). Cover with plastic wrap. The chicken can marinate for 2 hours in the refrigerator, or can be cooked immediately.

Microwave chicken, covered, on high for 6 minutes. Then, turn each piece over and baste with pan juices. Sprinkle each piece with remaining half of the dry spices. Cover again with plastic wrap and microwave on high for 6 more minutes.

Next, grill the chicken, covered, on a gas barbecue or grill for 5 minutes. Then, turn chicken pieces over and baste liberally with pan juices (saved after microwaving). Much of the juices and spices will fall onto the charcoal or lava rocks. This helps to cool the chicken during the last critical 5 minutes when the chicken could singe. The resulting flavored steam infuses the chicken with the flavor of the spices after grilling.

 Cover grill and cook for 5 more minutes (10 minutes total grilling time). Serve immediately.

Nutritional Analysis (per serving)

Calories	266	Carbohydrates	1.85 g
Calories from fat	37%	Dietary fiber	.393 g
Total fat	10.5 g	Cholesterol	118 mg
Protein..	39.0 g	Sodium	477 mg

Cioppino

SUSAN SISSON, SEATTLE

Serves 8

1 1/2 *cups green pepper, chopped*
1 1/2 *cups yellow onion, chopped*
3 *tablespoons olive oil*
3 *14-ounce cans tomatoes, including juice*
2 *tablespoons tomato paste*
2 *cups white wine*
1 1/2 *teaspoons basil*
1 1/2 *teaspoons oregano*
1 1/2 *teaspoons thyme*
2 *bay leaves*
3/4 *teaspoon hot red pepper flakes*
1/4 *cup parsley, chopped*
3/4 *pound shrimp, medium size*
24 *clams*
1 *pound halibut or cod, cut into*
     1 1/2-*inch pieces*
3/4 *pound scallops*

Combine green pepper, onion, and olive oil. Cook until soft. Add tomatoes, tomato paste, wine, basil, oregano, thyme, bay leaves, red pepper flakes, and parsley. Bring to a boil, then simmer, covered, for 1 1/2 hours.

Bring sauce back to a boil, then add shrimp, clams, halibut or cod, and scallops. Remove clams as they open, and simmer fish for 5 to 7 minutes. Stir in clams and serve.

Nutritional Analysis (per serving)

Calories	220	Carbohydrates	10.8 g
Calories from fat	28%	Dietary fiber	2.42 g
Total fat	7.01 g	Cholesterol	110 mg
Protein..	29.1 g	Sodium	429 mg

Coho Fillet

RUTH MATTESON, SEATTLE

Serves 4

4 *Coho fillets equaling approximately 1 1/2*
     pounds, skinned and boned
1 *large onion, thinly sliced*
2 *tablespoons olive oil*

1 green pepper, thinly sliced
1/2 red pepper, sliced
1 large clove garlic, minced
1 large tomato, or 2 medium, thinly sliced
2 tablespoons lemon juice
2 teaspoons dried basil
pepper to taste
salt to taste, optional

In a large skillet, cook onion in oil over medium heat until onion is translucent. Add green pepper, red pepper, and garlic. Cook for 3 or 4 minutes. Lay tomato over vegetables. Continue cooking for 2 or 3 more minutes. Most of liquid will have evaporated.

Arrange fillets over vegetables, folding thinner tail part under thicker forward section. Sprinkle with lemon juice, basil, salt, and pepper. Cover. Heat to near boil, reduce heat to simmer.

Simmer, covered, for 10 minutes. Salmon will flake easily and should have an opaque, milky appearance around edges. Serve immediately.

Nutritional Analysis (per serving)

Calories 365	Carbohydrates .... 7.19 g
Calories from fat 52%	Dietary fiber .... 1.79 g
Total fat .... 21.1 g	Cholesterol .... 111 mg
Protein. .... 36.1 g	Sodium .... 89.1 mg

Curry & Fruit Chicken Salad

DEE SANDLAND, OLYMPIA

Serves 6

1 medium size red apple, cored
3 cups chicken, cooked, boned, skinned, and cut into bite size pieces
1 1/2 cups celery, thinly sliced
3/4 cup dry roasted salted peanuts, halved
1/2 cup raisins
1 8-ounce can sliced pineapple, drained
6 to 8 large lettuce leaves, washed and crisped

2 tablespoons minced candied ginger, optional

Curry Dressing

1 cup sour cream, or plain yogurt, or half of each
2 tablespoons lemon juice
1 teaspoon dry dill weed
1 1/2 teaspoons curry powder

Cut apple lengthwise into thin slices. Combine apple, chicken, celery, 1/2 cup peanuts, and raisins, and cover.

Blend dressing ingredients together. Toss salad with dressing. Arrange lettuce leaves on dinner plates. Place one pineapple slice on each leaf. Top with chicken salad. Sprinkle with remaining peanuts and candied ginger.

Nutritional Analysis (per serving)

Calories 364	Carbohydrates .... 27.1 g
Calories from fat 43%	Dietary fiber .... 4.34 g
Total fat .... 18.1 g	Cholesterol .... 66.8 mg
Protein.. .... 26.7 g	Sodium .... 108 mg

Curried Rice & Turkey Salad

FRANCES TREVISAN, SEATTLE

Serves 4

2 cups cooked turkey meat, diced
1/2 cup water
1 slice of onion
celery top
dash of salt
1/2 teaspoon ground black pepper
2 cups cold cooked rice, white or brown
1/2 green pepper chopped, fine
2 tablespoons parsley, chopped
2 or 3 green onions, chopped
1 cup celery, diced
1 cup fresh pineapple
pepper to taste

Dressing

2 tablespoons olive oil
1/4 cup rice or wine vinegar

2 tablespoons of lemon juice
2 or 3 cloves garlic, minced
1 tablespoon sugar
1 teaspoon curry powder

Place turkey, water, onion, celery, salt and pepper in a 2-quart saucepan. Bring to boil and simmer for 30 minutes. Drain off broth. Cool turkey.

Mix together dressing ingredients. In a large bowl, combine turkey, rice, green pepper, parsley, green onions, celery, and pineapple. Chill. Just before serving pour dressing over salad and mix well. If desired, garnish with salad greens, green pepper, and tomato.

Nutritional Analysis (per serving)

Calories 358	Carbohydrates .... 44.5 g
Calories from fat 24%	Dietary fiber .... 3.09 g
Total fat .... 9.71 g	Cholesterol .... 48.5 mg
Protein.. .... 24.1 g	Sodium .... 79.8 mg

Dilled Salmon

RAY RUHLEN, SEATTLE

Serves 4

4 coho salmon steaks, total weight 2 pounds

Marinade:

¹/₂ cup orange juice
¹/₄ cup lemon juice
¹/₄ cup finely chopped fresh or 1 tablespoon
*   dried dill*
¹/₈ cup finely chopped fresh or 2 teaspoons
*   dried rosemary*

Sauce:

1 cup nonfat yogurt
3 tablespoons low calorie mayonnaise
¹/₄ cup finely chopped fresh or 1 tablespoon
*   dried dill*

Stir marinade ingredients together and pour over salmon steaks. Marinate for 45 minutes. Remove steaks from marinade and brush off herbs. Grill over coals or under broiler, turning once. After turning, spread sauce over top

surface when grilling. If broiling, spread on top when second side is almost cooked. Broil with sauce until done. Serve, with leftover sauce on side.

Nutritional Analysis (per serving)

Calories 343	Carbohydrates .... 11.7 g
Calories from fat 35%	Dietary fiber .... 0.390 g
Total fat .... 13.2 g	Cholesterol .... 73.2 mg
Protein.. .... 42.7 g	Sodium .... 190 mg

Easy Raisin-Curried Delight Fish

SALLY M. COLE, SEATTLE

Serves 4

2 pounds cod, sole, or halibut
¹/₂ cup mayonnaise (low calorie)
1 ¹/₂ teaspoon curry powder
¹/₄ teaspoon garlic powder
¹/₃ cup raisins

Mix mayonnaise, curry, garlic, and raisins in small bowl. Place fish in shallow, lightly-greased glass baking dish and spread mixture evenly over fish. Bake, uncovered, at 375 degrees for 12 to 23 minutes, depending upon thickness of fish, until fish flakes with a fork.

Serve with rice and sautéed vegetables.

Nutritional Analysis (per serving)

Calories 278	Carbohydrates .... 14.0 g
Calories from fat 24%	Dietary fiber .... 0.902 g
Total fat .... 7.39 g	Cholesterol .... 101 mg
Protein.. .... 38.0 g	Sodium .... 283 mg

Gulf Coast Caper

LARZ NEISES, SPOKANE

Serves 6

1 tablespoon canola oil
1 medium onion, diced
2 jalapeno peppers, seeded and diced
3 garlic cloves, minced
1¹/₂ pounds tomatoes (5 medium), peeled
*   and chopped*

2 bay leaves
2 tablespoons capers
12 Spanish-style green olives, pitted and
    sliced
2 pounds red snapper or cod fillets
$1/2$ lime

Saute onion, garlic, and pepper in hot
oil. Cook until tender, but not browned.
Add tomatoes, bay leaves, capers, and
olives. Bring to a boil and then reduce
heat. Simmer sauce 10 minutes,
uncovered. While sauce is cooking,
place fish fillets in a large skillet and
squeeze juice from $1/2$ lime over the top
of the fish. When sauce is finished
cooking, pour over fish and bring to a
boil. Reduce heat to simmer and cook
10 minutes or until fish flakes easily.

Nutritional Analysis (per serving)

Calories 212	Carbohydrates .... 8.61 g
Calories from fat 25%	Dietary fiber .... 2.77 g
Total fat .... 5.82 g	Cholesterol .... 53.3 mg
Protein.. .... 31.5 g	Sodium .... 428 mg

Joe's Ketchikan Burritos

JOE SUNDAL, SEATTLE

Serves 12

1 $1/2$ pounds halibut cheeks
$1/2$ cup salsa, mild, medium or hot
1 small bunch cilantro, leaves only, finely
    chopped
12 flour tortillas, burrito size works best
1 large tomato, diced
1 small head lettuce, shredded
$1/2$ pound cheddar cheese, grated
1 bunch green onions, sliced

Hand shred halibut cheeks into fine
strips. Simmer shredded halibut cheeks
and half of the cilantro in salsa until
flaky, about 15 minutes. Drain excess
liquid.

Heat tortillas in oven or microwave
until warm. Fill warm tortillas with

halibut. Add prepared tomato, lettuce,
onion, and cheese. Top with additional
cilantro and salsa, if desired. Fold
tortillas burrito style.

Nutritional Analysis (per serving)

Calories 298	Carbohydrates .... 32.6 g
Calories from fat 35%	Dietary fiber .... 2.16 g
Total fat .... 11.9 g	Cholesterol .... 34.5 mg
Protein.. .... 17.0 g	Sodium .... 368 mg

Leila's Oriental Chicken

LEILA HICKMAN, ROCKFORD

Serves 6

1 chicken, skinned and cut up
3 tablespoons honey
3 tablespoons low sodium soy sauce
1 tablespoon chicken broth
1 clove garlic, crushed
3 green onions, chopped
$1/2$ green pepper, cut in strips
1 cup carrots, cut in small strips and
    microwaved until tender/crisp, reserving
    water for sauce
$1/2$ small can sliced water chestnuts
$1^1/2$ tablespoons cornstarch
4 tablespoons sugar, part brown
Pineapple juice
2 tablespoons vinegar

In pan, cover chicken with foil and bake
45 minutes at 350 degrees. Add honey,
soy sauce, chicken broth, garlic and
green onions. Bake another 10 to 15
minutes, watching closely. Set aside.

Sauté green pepper, carrots and water
chestnuts in a very small amount of corn
oil in skillet, just until heated through.
Set aside to add to heated sauce.

Combine cornstarch and vinegar.
Combine water from carrots with
pineapple juice to make $1^1/2$ cups,
adding water if necessary. Combine this
with vinegar. Gradually add

cornstarch/sugar mixture to pineapple juice mixture.

Microwave until fairly thick and transparent, stirring frequently. Adjust sugar and vinegar to taste. Add vegetables and pour over chicken.

Nutritional Analysis (per serving)

Calories 265	Carbohydrates .... 32.7 g
Calories from fat 12%	Dietary fiber .... 1.49 g
Total fat .... 3.64 g	Cholesterol .... 79.6 mg
Protein.. .... 25.5 g	Sodium .... 632 mg

Linguine with Mussels & Capers

LARRY LUND, SEATTLE

Serves 6

3 dozen mussels
3 tablespoons coarsely chopped shallots
1 tablespoon capers
1 1/2 cups of canned Italian tomatoes
3 tablespoons olive oil or safflower oil
2 teaspoons chopped garlic
3 tablespoons finely chopped Italian parsley
1 tablespoon chopped fresh basil (or substitute any of your favorite herbs, dry or fresh)
1/2 cup dry white wine
1 1/2 pounds linguine (or substitute another pasta)
pepper to taste

Wash, scrub and remove beards from mussels. In a large skillet, heat 2 tablespoons of the oil, add 1 tablespoon of the shallots and 1/4 cup of the wine, and over medium hot heat cook the mussels until they open. Remove from the pan, take them out of their shell and reserve, together with the liquid, in a small bowl.

In a medium-sized saucepan, sauté 2 tablespoons shallots in the remaining oil over medium heat until translucent.

Add garlic and cook until lightly browned.

Add tomatoes and basil, together with the remaining 1/4 cup of wine. Bring to a boil, then turn down heat and simmer for 15 minutes. Add the juice of mussels and simmer an additional 5 minutes. Add the mussels and capers and heat briefly.

Cook and drain pasta, then toss with the parsley and place on a serving platter. Spoon the sauce over the pasta and serve.

Nutritional Analysis (per serving)

Calories 396	Carbohydrates .... 57.0 g
Calories from fat 47%	Dietary fiber .... 6.67 g
Total fat .... 29.2 g	Cholesterol .... 50.4 mg
Protein.. .... 18.0 g	Sodium .... 318 mg

Oyster Stuffed Potatoes

RUTH KRAUSS, M.D., SEATTLE

Serves 4

2 large baking potatoes
1 medium onion
a few scallions
1 pint medium oysters, fresh
1/8 pound small cooked shrimp
1/4 cup skim milk
1 to 2 ounces grated cheddar cheese
black pepper, thyme, sage, etc.

Bake the potatoes in 400 degree oven until done. Cut each potato in half and scoop out insides. Save shells.

Slice or chop the onion. Braise it in a medium saucepan in a bit of water until almost translucent. Add the potato insides and mash. Add enough milk to moisten the potatoes slightly. Slice the oysters in thirds and add to the mashed potatoes. Chop the scallions and add. Add the shrimp. Add spices to taste.

Heat on stove top until the mixture is warm throughout.

Spoon the mixture into the potato shells. Top with grated cheese, if desired. Bake for 15 minutes at 350 degrees.

Nutritional Analysis (per serving)

Calories 271	Carbohydrates .... 34.8 g
Calories from fat 23%	Dietary fiber .... 3.37 g
Total fat .... 6.89 g	Cholesterol .... 98.2 mg
Protein.. .... 17.5 g	Sodium .... 234 mg

Pineapple & Orange Chicken Breast Delite

JANE HINES, YAKIMA

Serves 4

1 8-ounce can pineapple chunks, packed in juice
1/2 cup chopped onion
1 teaspoon instant chicken bouillon granules
1 tablespoon low sodium soy sauce
1 tablespoon brown sugar or honey
1 tablespoon vinegar
2 whole medium chicken breasts, skinned, boned, and halved lengthwise
1 1/2 teaspoons cornstarch
2 tablespoons water
1 11-ounce can mandarin oranges, drained (juice pack)

Drain pineapple, reserving juice. Add enough water to juice to measure 1/2 cup. In large skillet combine pineapple liquid, onion, brown sugar or honey, vinegar, soy sauce, and bouillon granules. Bring to a boil. Add chicken and reduce heat. Cover tightly and simmer for 30 minutes, turning chicken after 15 minutes.

Remove chicken and set aside. Combine corn starch and water; stir into skillet. Cook and stir until thickened and bubbly. Add pineapple, orange sections and chicken; heat through. Serve with hot rice.

Nutritional Analysis (per serving)

Calories 170	Carbohydrates .... 24.8 g
Calories from fat 9%	Dietary fiber .... 1.85 g
Total fat .... 1.79 g	Cholesterol .... 36.7 mg
Protein.. .... 14.6 g	Sodium .... 596 mg

Papaya Broiled Fish

SELMA COLE, BOTHELL

Serves 6

2 pounds Mahi-Mahi, tuna or snapper fillets, 1 inch thick
1 ripe papaya
1/2-inch piece of fresh ginger
1 clove garlic
1 lime

Peel papaya, discard seeds, and cut into chunks. Zest the skin of the lime to equal 1/2 teaspoon. Juice the lime. Peel ginger, and slice. Put slices in a garlic press a few at a time and press to extract juice. Put papaya chunks, lime juice, ginger juice, and pressed garlic in a blender and blend on "chop" setting. Reserve zest of the lime.

This makes about 1 1/2 cups of basting sauce. Use about 1/2 cup for this recipe. Remaining sauce can be sealed in a jar and refrigerated. It will keep for about a month.

Pre-heat broiler. Lightly oil broiler pan. Place fish fillets skin side down on pan. Broil 4 inches from heat source for 10 to 15 minutes, or until fish flakes easily when tested with a fork. Baste fish with the sauce after 5 minutes and again at 10 minutes, or just prior to the fish being done. Remove to a warmed serving dish and sprinkle zest of lime over filets.

Nutritional Analysis (per serving)

Calories 201	Carbohydrates .... 1.87 g
Calories from fat 12%	Dietary fiber .... 0.297 g
Total fat .... 2.63 g	Cholesterol .... 71.1 mg
Protein.. .... 39.9 g	Sodium .... 86.7 mg

Party Chicken Rolls

ELLIDA K. LATHROP, BONNEY LAKE

Serves 8

2 chicken breasts, washed, skinned, boned,
     halved, and pounded flat
1 6 ³/₄-ounce can deviled ham
ground pepper
dried oregano
dried basil
dried chopped parsley

Spread each chicken breast with ¹/₄ can
deviled ham. Sprinkle lightly with
spices. Roll up. Place the 4 chicken rolls
seam side down in a glass baking dish
that has been sprayed with non-stick
vegetable spray. Bake uncovered for 30
to 40 minutes at 350 degrees. Cover and
refrigerate, or may be frozen for later
use. To serve, slice each chicken roll into
8 slices and serve with rye rounds or
sesame crackers.

Nutritional Analysis (per serving)

Calories	87.1	Carbohydrates	2.54 g
Calories from fat	47%	Dietary fiber	0.030 g
Total fat	4.46 g	Cholesterol	27.0 mg
Protein..	8.75 g	Sodium	234 mg

Pockets
Full of Chicken

CATHERINE A. NOLAN, SEATTLE

Serves 8

1 medium sized onion, chopped
2 cloves garlic, minced
1 green pepper, thinly sliced or chopped
1 red pepper, thinly sliced or chopped
1 small zucchini, thinly sliced
1 4-ounce can diced green chilies
1 tablespoon oil, polyunsaturated or
     nonsaturated
1 pound slightly frozen boneless, skinless
     chicken meat
1 ¹/₂ teaspoons ground cumin
1 tablespoon flour
¹/₃ cup salsa

1 teaspoon oregano, dried
1 teaspoon basil, dried
¹/₈ teaspoon black pepper
1 package whole wheat pita bread (4 pitas)

Slice each pita in half making a total of 8
pockets. Cut slightly frozen chicken
meat into thin slices. Sauté onion, garlic,
green pepper, red pepper, and small
zucchini in 1 tablespoon of oil. Stir in
cumin, oregano, basil, and black pepper.

Sauté chicken slices with mixed
vegetables. When chicken has cooked,
move mixture to the side of the pan.
Slowly add flour and stir constantly
until sauce thickens. Add green chilies
and salsa. Scoop mixture into the pita
bread. Serve immediately

Nutritional Analysis (per serving)

Calories	202	Carbohydrates	22.3 g
Calories from fat	25%	Dietary fiber	1.90 g
Total fat	5.60 g	Cholesterol	35.2 mg
Protein..	15.7 g	Sodium	210 mg

Scallops & Spinach

JULIA A. JOSE, SPOKANE

Serves 4

1 pound scallops, rinsed
2 tablespoons lemon juice
2 bunches fresh spinach, washed and
     coarsely torn or chopped, or 2 boxes
     frozen spinach, thawed
1 cup green onions, sliced
2 cloves garlic, minced
¹/₃ to ¹/₂ pound fresh mushrooms, sliced
1 tablespoon vegetable oil
1 15-ounce container of lowfat ricotta cheese
2 cups cooked rice
Parmesan cheese, optional

Add lemon juice to scallops and
marinate while fixing rest of ingredients.

 In a large skillet or wok steam spinach,
onions and garlic using only the water
clinging to spinach. When spinach is
limp, push to sides of pan.

Add 1 tablespoon oil in center and pour in scallops and juice. Stir-fry until almost cooked through.

Add mushrooms and continue cooking for another 2 minutes. Add ricotta and mix all ingredients together gently. Reduce heat.

Cover and steam for 3 to 5 minutes, or until cheese melts and flavors blend. Season with pepper and a touch of salt or salt substitute. Serve over rice. Add a sprinkle of Parmesan cheese if desired.

Nutritional Analysis (per serving)

Calories	496	Carbohydrates	55.2 g
Calories from fat	24%	Dietary fiber	6.98 g
Total fat	13.7 g	Cholesterol	70.3 mg
Protein..	40.4 g	Sodium	417 mg

Slim Elegance Salad

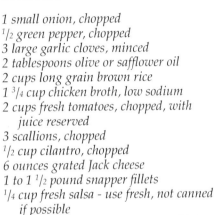

MARTHA C. LEA, SHELTON

Serves 4

Salad

1 6 1/2-ounce can water pack white tuna, chilled and drained
1 8-ounce can chunk pineapple, chilled and drained. Save 3 tablespoons of juice
1/2 cup celery, thinly sliced
1 green onion, 1 inch of green top included, finely chopped
4 romaine lettuce leaves
4 slices whole wheat bread

Dressing

3 tablespoons low-calorie mayonnaise
3 tablespoons pineapple juice

Combine tuna, pineapple, celery, and green onion. Mix together mayonnaise and pineapple juice. Toss salad lightly with dressing. Divide into four portions and mound on romaine lettuce leaves. Cut each slice of whole wheat bread into four strips and double toast them. Garnish salad with toast strips.

Nutritional Analysis (per serving)

Calories	124	Carbohydrates	11.2 g
Calories from fat	19%	Dietary fiber	1.20 g
Total fat	2.67 g	Cholesterol	28.7 mg
Protein..	14.1 g	Sodium	234 mg

Snapper Salsa

MARY SUE GALVIN, SEATTLE

Serves 5 to 6

1 small onion, chopped
1/2 green pepper, chopped
3 large garlic cloves, minced
2 tablespoons olive or safflower oil
2 cups long grain brown rice
1 3/4 cup chicken broth, low sodium
2 cups fresh tomatoes, chopped, with juice reserved
3 scallions, chopped
1/2 cup cilantro, chopped
6 ounces grated Jack cheese
1 to 1 1/2 pound snapper fillets
1/4 cup fresh salsa - use fresh, not canned if possible
1/2 lemon, or equivalent amount of juice

Sauté onion, green pepper and garlic in oil. Add rice and stir 1 to 2 minutes until grains become opaque. Add chicken broth and juice from tomatoes. Liquid should measure 3 to 3 1/4 cups. Add 2 tablespoons chopped cilantro. Simmer for 40 to 60 minutes or until the rice is done. Add extra water if needed.

Chop scallions and grate cheese. Place tomatoes in saucepan and mix in salsa until desired spiciness is reached. Bring to a simmer; you may want to add extra garlic and cilantro here if salsa is not spicy enough.

When rice is done, transfer to baking/serving dish. Arrange fillets on top. Squeeze over juice from 1 lemon. Bake for 10 minutes at 400 degrees per each 1 inch thickness of fish. Pour tomato salsa mixture on top of fish, then sprinkle on cheese. Return to oven and bake until cheese melts.

Nutritional Analysis (per serving)

Calories 508	Carbohydrates .... 52.3 g
Calories from fat 30%	Dietary fiber .... 3.35 g
Total fat .... 16.5 g	Cholesterol .... 66.2 mg
Protein.. .... 36.2 g	Sodium .... 448 mg

Steamed Halibut in Foil

JULIE VELA, REDMOND

Serves 4

2 pounds of halibut, in single slices
4 small carrots, cut into julienne strips
4 green onions, cut lengthwise into julienne strips
1 can Italian plum tomatoes, drained, cut into small pieces
2 teaspoons finely chopped, peeled fresh ginger root
2 teaspoons margarine
1 tablespoon lemon juice
2 teaspoons sesame oil

Place halibut on piece of foil large enough to enclose fish and vegetables. Top with carrot, green onion, tomato, and ginger root. Dot with margarine. Sprinkle with lemon juice and sesame oil.

Lift up 2 long edges of foil and bring up and over the fish; fold to make tight seal. Seal ends. Place on cookie sheet for 17 to 20 minutes at 475 degrees.

Note: This can be divided into 4 servings, each with own foil packet.

Nutritional Analysis (per serving)

Calories 338	Carbohydrates .... 9.37 g
Calories from fat 27%	Dietary fiber .... 2.68 g
Total fat .... 10.3 g	Cholesterol .... 81.4 mg
Protein.. .... 45.3 g	Sodium .... 294 mg

Susan's Oriental Chicken

SUSAN LEAVITT, SEATTLE

Serves 4

4 chicken thighs, skin removed
1 6-ounce can apricot juice
1 6-ounce can pineapple juice
2 tablespoons soy sauce
4 tablespoons white vinegar
1 large clove garlic, minced
¹/₄ teaspoon 5 spice
4 tablespoons minced onion
canned apricots, peaches or sliced oranges, optional
fresh parsley, optional

Arrange chicken on a rack and broil 4 inches from heat for 5 minutes, turning once. Place chicken in a shallow pan. Reduce oven temperature to 350 degrees.

Combine all other ingredients and pour over chicken. Bake chicken for 30 to 40 minutes or until done. Sauce should be thick.

Arrange chicken on platter and pour sauce over. Dish may be garnished with canned apricots, peaches, or sliced oranges. Top with parsley.

Nutritional Analysis (per serving)

Calories 168	Carbohydrates .... 14.7 g
Calories from fat 31%	Dietary fiber .... 0.583 g
Total fat .... 5.78 g	Cholesterol .... 49.0 mg
Protein.. .... 14.4 g	Sodium .... 563 mg

Stuffed Peppers

MOLLY McLAUGHLIN, BELLINGHAM

Serves 4

2 large green peppers, parboiled
1 pound lean ground turkey
1 cup chopped onion
1 clove garlic, minced
1 cup tomato sauce
¹/₂ cup raisins

2 teaspoons chili powder
¹/₂ teaspoons cinnamon
¹/₈ teaspoon cloves
4 cups stewed tomatoes
2 cups cooked brown rice

Cut peppers in half, removing seeds and stems. Parboil peppers by plunging them into boiling water for approximately 8 minutes, then plunge immediately into cold water. Drain.

Brown meat slowly in a non-stick frying pan, breaking into small chunks. Add onion and garlic, and cook for 2 minutes. Add tomato sauce, raisins, spices, and stewed tomatoes. Simmer for 15 minutes.

Place peppers, open side up, in baking dish. Pour filling into and around peppers. Bake for 15 minutes at 350 degrees. Serve with rice.

Nutritional Analysis (per serving)

Calories	461	Carbohydrates	61.6 g
Calories from fat	24%	Dietary fiber	8.00 g
Total fat	12.9 g	Cholesterol	71.4 mg
Protein..	29.2 g	Sodium	887 mg

Summer Chicken with Lemon & Basil

ELLIDA K. LATHROP, BONNEY LAKE

Serves 6

3 chicken breasts or 6 hindquarters

Marinade

¹/₂ cup lemon juice
1 tablespoon almond or avocado oil
¹/₂ cup fresh basil leaves, chopped
2 to 3 tablespoons fresh tarragon leaves
4 cloves garlic, peeled and crushed
1 tablespoon fresh ground pepper
2 teaspoons grated fresh lemon rind

Wash, skin, and dry chicken breasts and hindquarters. Mix marinade ingredients in a plastic bag and add chicken parts.

Let sit 4 hours to overnight in refrigerator.

Heat barbecue grill to hot, spray a wire basket with non-stick vegetable spray. Place drained chicken parts in basket and save remaining marinade for basting. Grill until chicken starts to brown, 10 to 15 minutes.

Reduce heat to medium-low if using gas barbecue, or move chicken away from the hottest coals. Continue cooking, turning every 10 minutes. Baste with marinade each time chicken is turned. Cook until fork tender and juices run clear. Sprinkle on chopped fresh basil before serving if desired.

Nutritional Analysis (per serving)

Calories	114	Carbohydrates	5.85 g
Calories from fat	31%	Dietary fiber	1.06 g
Total fat	4.11 g	Cholesterol	36.5 mg
Protein..	14.5 g	Sodium	35.3 mg

Tarragon-Dijon Chicken

JANETTE M. HURSH, COPALIS BEACH

Serves 6

6 chicken breasts (about 4 ounces each), skinned, rinsed, and patted dry
no-stick cooking spray
²/₃ cup unsweetened pineapple juice
¹/₂ cup white wine Worchestershire sauce
1 tablespoon country-style Dijon mustard
¹/₂ teaspoon crushed, dried tarragon

Spray 9-x-13-inch baking dish with no-stick cooking spray. Place chicken breasts flesh side down in baking dish. Combine remaining ingredients and pour over chicken. Cover snugly with aluminum foil, sealing edges.

Bake one hour, 10 minutes at 350 degrees. During final 10 minutes, remove foil and turn the chicken flesh side up. Remove chicken breasts to serving platter. Strain the reserved juice and spoon over each piece before serving.

Nutritional Analysis (per serving)

Calories 158	Carbohydrates .... 4.02 g
Calories from fat 19%	Dietary fiber .... 0.103 g
Total fat .... 3.11 g	Cholesterol .... 72.2 mg
Protein.. .... 26.6 g	Sodium .... 243 mg

Thai Shrimp

S.M. ESTVANIK

Serves 6

2 pounds large shrimp
juice from 1 lime
1 tablespoon paprika
$^1/_2$ teaspoon cayenne or 1 to 2 chopped
    Thai chiles
$^1/_4$ cup fresh coriander, chopped

Clean shrimp and toss with lime juice. Add seasonings and marinate for $^1/_2$ hour. Broil for 5 to 8 minutes.

Nutritional Analysis (per serving)

Calories 127	Carbohydrates .... 1.20 g
Calories from fat 11%	Dietary fiber .... 0.332 g
Total fat .... 1.51 g	Cholesterol .... 240 mg
Protein.. .... 25.9 g	Sodium .... 276 mg

Dairy Products

▲▲▲▲▲▲▲▲▲▲▲▲▲▲▲▲

Dairy Products

Custards, puddings, ice cream, sauces, dips, milkshakes, quiches, cheeses, yogurts. Are they good for you? You bet. They're full of protein and calcium. Unfortunately, they're also full of fat and cholesterol. How can you continue to enjoy dairy products and stay healthy at the same time? The answer is simple: Use the low fat variety.

Most often that means making substitutions and reading labels. Take cottage cheese, for instance. A one-half cup serving of creamed cottage cheese contains 5 grams of fat and 17 milligrams of cholesterol. By comparing labels you'll find that low fat, 1-percent cottage cheese has only 1.2 grams of fat and 5 milligrams of cholesterol.

Similar savings can be made with milk. A one-cup serving of whole milk provides approximately 8 grams of fat, while a one-cup serving of skim milk has less than 1 gram. In between is 2-percent milk, which contains 5 grams of fat per serving.

Of all dairy foods, cheese may be the one item people love most. You don't have to give it up completely. Just make sure that you save the high-fat cheeses—cheddar, jack, Swiss, Bleu, and of course, Brie—for the once-in-a-while, special occasions. For everyday use, switch to the lower-fat cheeses—Mozarrellas made from part-skim milk, part-skim ricotta, and low fat, 1-percent cottage cheese.

You can also experiment by reducing the amount of cheese in your favorite recipes. Instead of sprinkling a cup of grated cheese on top of a casserole, try using a half-cup or less. Sample some of the "diet" cheeses or reduced-fat cheeses and see how you like them.

One area of confusion for many is the butter vs. margarine controversy. What's the difference? In caloric value, not much, but butter and margarine do have different kinds of fat. Butter is high in saturated fat and cholesterol. Margarine, depending on the brand, is lower in saturated fat and cholesterol and higher in the preferred fats—polyunsaturated and monounsaturated. Most brands of margarine are cholesterol-free. Stick margarine tends to have a higher saturated fat content than tub margarine. Again, read the labels and choose a margarine that lists liquid oil as the first ingredient—either safflower oil, sunflower oil, or corn oil is preferred.

▲▲▲▲▲▲▲▲▲▲▲▲▲▲▲▲▲

Try the following cooking and shopping tips for buying and cooking with dairy products:

◆ Substitute plain, nonfat yogurt in many dishes that call for sour cream or mayonnaise. Stroganoff, salad dressings, and dips, for instance, adapt well to yogurt.

◆ Try adding a pinch of sugar, honey, or sugar substitute to nonfat yogurt if it tastes too tart or bitter for you.

◆ Boost the protein and calcium content of meals without adding extra fat by adding nonfat dry milk powder to soups, casseroles, mashed potatoes—even your glass of milk.

◆ Use medium heat when cooking with cheese. This advice also applies to microwave cooking. Cheese will melt more evenly and you'll avoid a rubbery texture.

◆ Move ice cream to the "once in a while" list. As a substitute, try fruit juice bars, sorbets, sherbets, or ice milk—which has only half the fat content of ice cream.

◆ Skip buttering your morning toast or pancakes. Try nonfat yogurt or low fat cottage cheese with cinnamon or jam instead.

Keep an open mind, do some experimenting and use the following recipes to declare war on fat.

Almost Cheesecake

MARTHA SCHAEFER, LYNNWOOD

Serves 8

Crust

³/₄ cup graham cracker crumbs
3 tablespoons margarine

Filling

4 cups low fat cottage cheese
2 large eggs
2 large egg whites
¹/₂ cup sugar
1 teaspoon vanilla
¹/₂ teaspoon grated orange rind
¹/₂ teaspoon grated lemon rind
¹/₂ cup low fat plain yogurt
¹/₂ cup low fat milk
¹/₄ cup all-purpose flour

For crust, mix softened margarine and
crumbs together. Press mixture onto the
bottom and partly up the sides of a
greased 9-inch baking dish or spring
form mold. Bake for 10 minutes at 350
degrees. Let cool.

In a food processor, blend filling
ingredients together in the order listed.
Pour the cheesecake mixture into the
prepared crust. Bake for 1 hour, at 350
degrees or until the sides are just
beginning to brown and the center is
still soft. Allow to cool in oven, with
door slightly propped open, for
3 hours. Chill.

Top individual servings with slightly
mashed fresh or frozen berries.

Nutritional Analysis (per serving)

Calories	277	Carbohydrates	32.0 g
Calories from fat	24%	Dietary fiber	0.883 g
Total fat	7.27 g	Cholesterol	63.8 mg
Protein	20.6 g	Sodium	627 mg

Baked Eggplant & Ricotta Cheese

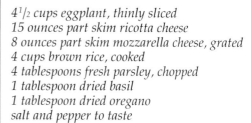

SUSAN FLEAGLE, SEATTLE

Serves 8

4¹/₂ cups eggplant, thinly sliced
15 ounces part skim ricotta cheese
8 ounces part skim mozzarella cheese, grated
4 cups brown rice, cooked
4 tablespoons fresh parsley, chopped
1 tablespoon dried basil
1 tablespoon dried oregano
salt and pepper to taste

Broil eggplant slices with skin
remaining until tender, turning when
golden.

Place ¹/₂ eggplant on bottom of 10" x 14"
greased pan. Add ¹/₂ ricotta, then ¹/₂
cooked brown rice. Sprinkle ¹/₂ parsley,
basil, oregano and salt/pepper onto
rice. Top with ¹/₂ grated mozzarella
cheese.

Repeat layers once more, using up all
ingredients. Cover with foil and bake
for 45 minutes at 350 degrees.

Nutritional Analysis (per serving)

Calories	285	Carbohydrates	32.2 g
Calories from fat	31%	Dietary fiber	3.52 g
Total fat	9.60 g	Cholesterol	31.4 mg
Protein	16.8 g	Sodium	219 mg

Cheesy Italian Pie

HAZEL JEAN LAWS, OLYMPIA

Serves 6

1 10-ounce package frozen chopped spinach
1 cup mozzarella cheese, shredded
Egg substitute equal to 4 eggs
1¹/₂ cups nonfat milk
¹/₂ teaspoon Italian seasoning
1 cup biscuit mix
¹/₄ cup parmesan cheese

Cook spinach according to package
directions, drain well. Press spinach

evenly in bottom of a greased 10-inch quiche pan. Sprinkle with mozzarella cheese.

Stir together eggs, milk, biscuit mix and Italian seasoning. Beat with rotary beater until well combined. Pour over mixture in quiche pan. Sprinkle with parmesan cheese.

Bake at 350 degrees for 30 to 35 minutes or until knife inserted near center comes out clean.

Nutritional Analysis (per serving)

Calories 258	Carbohydrates .... 16.5 g
Calories from fat 39%	Dietary fiber .... 1.26 g
Total fat .... 8.61 g	Cholesterol .... 25.4 mg
Protein .... 19.8 g	Sodium .... 610 mg

Cheese Spread

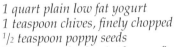

SELMA COLE, BOTHELL

Makes 6 ¹/₂-cup servings

1 quart plain low fat yogurt
1 teaspoon chives, finely chopped
¹/₂ teaspoon poppy seeds
¹/₂ teaspoon fresh mint leaves, finely chopped

Place 3 layers of cheese cloth in a colander large enough to hold the yogurt. Put the yogurt into the lined colander. Cover with another piece of cheese cloth. Suspend the colander over a pan at least 2 inches deeper than the bottom of the colander. Place in the refrigerator for 8 to 10 hours, or until the drained yogurt is the consistency of cream cheese. Turn the yogurt-cheese into a bowl. Add the remaining ingredients. Mix well. Store in a covered container in the refrigerator. Use as a sandwich spread or on crackers. Keeps well for two weeks.

Nutritional Analysis (per serving)

Calories 97.4	Carbohydrates .... 10.7 g
Calories from fat 23%	Dietary fiber .... 0.021 g
Total fat .... 2.42 g	Cholesterol .... 9.33 mg
Protein .... 7.98 g	Sodium .... 106 mg

Chilled Cheese & Huckleberries

LINDA DOBNEY, COLBERT

Serves 4

1 cup low fat cottage cheese
1 tablespoon lemon juice
¹/₄ cup sugar
1 cup nonfat plain yogurt
2 cups fresh or frozen huckleberries or other fresh berries
2 tablespoons sugar

Put cottage cheese, lemon juice, ¹/₄ cup sugar and yogurt in blender. Whip until smooth. Freeze in 5-x-8-inch bread pan until edges are firm. Remove from freezer and stir well. Return to freezer for about an hour or until soft-frozen.

Mix berries with 2 tablespoons sugar. Spoon chilled cheese into dessert goblets. Top with huckleberries.

Nutritional Analysis (per serving)

Calories 197	Carbohydrates .... 35.6 g
Calories from fat 7%	Dietary fiber .... 1.96 g
Total fat .... 1.48 g	Cholesterol .... 5.75 mg
Protein .... 11.5 g	Sodium .... 278 mg

Cottage Cheese Cake

LUCILLE MIKKELSEN, RAINIER

Serves 6

1 envelope unflavored gelatin (1 tablespoon)
¹/₃ cup granulated sugar
¹/₁₆ teaspoon salt
2 tablespoons egg substitute
¹/₂ cup skim milk
1 teaspoon lemon juice
1 teaspoon grated lemon rind
1 teaspoon vanilla
1¹/₂ cups of 2 percent cottage cheese
whipped cream made from ¹/₃ cup dry powdered milk
¹/₃ cup ice water
1 tablespoon lemon juice

*For diabetic leave the sugar out and add 16
packets of sugar substitute to the cottage
cheese.*

Topping

*¹/₂ cup finely crumbled zwieback
1 teaspoon sugar
¹/₂ teaspoon cinnamon*

Place mixing beaters into small mixing
bowl and fill with water and ice cubes.
Set aside. Place gelatin, sugar, salt, egg
substitute and milk in 2 quart sauce pan.
Stir thoroughly. Bring just to boiling on
medium heat, stirring constantly.
Remove from heat. Stir in lemon juice,
rind and vanilla. Cool until mixture
mounds slightly when stirred.

Pour into blender, add cottage cheese
and whip on highest speed until
smooth. Pour back into original pan.
Measure out ¹/₃ cup ice water from cold
mixing bowl; discard excess.

Put the ¹/₃ cup water back into cold
bowl, add ¹/₃ cup powdered milk and 1
tablespoon lemon juice and whip at
highest speed until mixture holds peaks.
Fold into cottage cheese mixture.

Place half the topping in the bottom of a
two quart dish; pour in cheese cake
mixture and cover with remaining
topping. Refrigerate. Serve plain or
with frozen or fresh berries or other
fruit. Taste is very delicate.

Nutritional Analysis (per serving)

Calories 159	Carbohydrates .... 23.2 g
Calories from fat 10%	Dietary fiber .... 578 g
Total fat .... 1.76 g	Cholesterol .... 6.22 mg
Protein .... 12.5 g	Sodium .... 355 mg

Cottage Cheese &
Carrot Pancakes

Bob Heffernan, Seattle

Makes 12 4-inch pancakes, 6 servings of 2 each

*1 cup low fat cottage cheese
1 egg white
1 cup buttermilk
1 small jar baby's strained carrots
2 teaspoons honey
¹/₂ cup whole-wheat flour
¹/₂ cup all-purpose flour
2 tablespoons wheat germ
1 teaspoon baking powder
¹/₂ teaspoon baking soda*

Blend together cottage cheese, egg
white, buttermilk, carrots and honey. In
a separate bowl, combine all the dry
ingredients. Pour in the liquid mixture
and stir just enough to blend them.

For each pancake, pour ¹/₄ cup of batter
on a hot, greased griddle. Cook the
pancakes over moderate heat until they
are golden brown on the bottom and the
tops begin to bubble. Then flip them
over, and cook until the under side
browns.

Nutritional Analysis (per serving)

Calories 147	Carbohydrates .... 23.2 g
Calories from fat 10%	Dietary fiber .... 2.44 g
Total fat .... 1.59 g	Cholesterol .... 4.67 mg
Protein .... 10.1 g	Sodium .... 334 mg

Frozen Yogurt Salad

Tracy Nelson, Bothell

Serves 10

*1 32-ounce low fat plain yogurt
1 16-ounce can pineapple chunks, packed in
     juice
1 16-ounce can peaches, cut into small
     chunks, packed in juice
1 16-ounce can pears, cut into small chunks,
     packed in juice*

1 or 2 bananas, sliced
³/₄ cup sugar
¹/₄ cup nuts, optional

Drain fruit. Combine ingredients in casserole dish. Freeze. Take out 2 minutes before serving.

Nutritional Analysis (per serving)

Calories 225	Carbohydrates ....45.4 g
Calories from fat 13%	Dietary fiber ....2.27 g
Total fat ....3.43 g	Cholesterol ....5.60 mg
Protein ....6.05 g	Sodium ....68.8 mg

Four Cheese Manicotti

ELLIDA KIRK LATHROP, BONNEY LAKE

Serves 7

1 large package manicotti

Filling

¹/₂ cup low fat cottage cheese
¹/₂ cup low fat ricotta cheese
4 ounces low fat cream cheese
1 teaspoon dried basil, or 2 tablespoons fresh basil, chopped
1 teaspoon dried parsley flakes, or 2 tablespoons fresh parsley, finely chopped
¹/₂ teaspoon dried oregano, or 1 tablespoon fresh oregano, finely chopped
1 egg
¹/₂ teaspoon ground pepper
1 bunch fresh spinach, or one 10-ounce box frozen spinach, cooked, drained, stemmed, and finely chopped

Sauce

1 cup tomato vegetable juice
1 15-ounce can low sodium tomato sauce
2 tablespoons grated Asiago, Romano, or Parmesan cheese

Cook manicotti according to package directions, omitting salt. Drain and cool on kitchen towels.

Mix all filling ingredients together and stuff cooked manicotti with cheese

mixture. (Manicotti may be frozen at this point to cook later.)

Spray a 9-x-12-inch glass baking dish with non-stick vegetable spray. Pour in ¹/₂ of tomato vegetable juice and ¹/₂ of tomato sauce. Place stuffed manicotti in dish. Pour over remaining juice and sauce.

Cover dish with aluminium foil or glass lid. Bake for 30 minutes at 325 degrees. Uncover and sprinkle with grated cheese. Bake 10 or 15 minutes more, or until cheese melts and sauce is bubbly.

Nutritional Analysis (per serving)

Calories 219	Carbohydrates ....24.5 g
Calories from fat 36%	Dietary fiber ....3.13 g
Total fat ....9.07 g	Cholesterol ....55.6 mg
Protein ....11.6 g	Sodium ....691 mg

Healthy Milk Shake

ELLEN LEVACK, FEDERAL WAY

Serves 2

6 ounces orange juice, or other fruit juice
1 banana, plus a little water
1 cup frozen unsweetened strawberries
¹/₃ cup powdered nonfat milk

Blend ingredients thoroughly.

Nutritional Analysis (per serving)

Calories 157	Carbohydrates ....34.9 g
Calories from fat 3%	Dietary fiber ....3.43 g
Total fat ....0.609 g	Cholesterol ....1.98 mg
Protein ....5.45 g	Sodium ....64.2 mg

Liquid Yogurt

NORMA STEPETAK, AUBURN

Serves 4

1 cup nonfat plain yogurt
1 cup nonfat milk
1 cup frozen or fresh fruit
¹/₂ to 1 teaspoon vanilla

1 tablespoon brown sugar, granulated sugar, or honey

Mix yogurt, milk, fruit, and vanilla in blender on high speed for 30 seconds or until well mixed. Blend in sugar or honey.

Vanilla yogurt may be substituted. If used omit vanilla extract.

Nutritional Analysis (per serving)

Calories 74.5	Carbohydrates .... 10.3 g
Calories from fat 18%	Dietary fiber .... 0.967 g
Total fat .... 1.54 g	Cholesterol .... 6.00 mg
Protein .... 5.14 g	Sodium .... 71.2 mg

Orange-Ginger Carrot Soup

JULIE GOLDING, SEATTLE

Serves 4

1 cup raw carrots, grated
2 to 3 shallots, minced
1 tablespoon fresh ginger root, grated
2 tablespoons flour
1 tablespoon margarine
1 tablespoon safflower oil
1¹/₂ cups 2 percent milk
1 cup low sodium chicken broth
¹/₂ cup plain yogurt
¹/₂ teaspoon curry powder
juice of one fresh orange
1 teaspoon grated orange peel
1 tablespoon fresh cilantro, chopped

In a heavy bottomed skillet, saute shallots and ginger in margarine and oil for about 5 minutes until shallots are soft and translucent. Add flour and cook on low heat for 3 minutes. Add carrots and chicken broth. Whisk rapidly to incorporate flour mixture.

Cook over low heat for 10 minutes, stirring often to keep from sticking. Remove soup from heat and let cool for 5 minutes. Add milk and yogurt, whisking rapidly to blend ingredients. Cook slowly over low heat another 10

minutes, stirring until mixture thickens slightly. Add curry powder, orange juice, and orange peel. Add salt and pepper to taste. Serve hot with a sprinkle of cilantro on top.

Nutritional Analysis (per serving)

Calories 132	Carbohydrates .... 17.1 g
Calories from fat 31%	Dietary fiber .... 1.31 g
Total fat .... 4.71 g	Cholesterol .... 10.2 mg
Protein .... 6.0 g	Sodium .... 310 mg

Pineapple Torte

MARTHA Y. BURRIER, EVERETT

Serves 8

1³/₄ cup crushed pineapple
1 package lemon gelatin
¹/₃ cup sugar
1 cup skimmed evaporated milk, chilled
1 cup graham cracker crumbs

Place can of skimmed evaporated milk in refrigerator over night. Chill large bowl.

Place undrained pineapple in saucepan and bring to a boil. When thoroughly hot, remove from heat. Stir in gelatin until dissolved. Stir in sugar. Set aside until mixture becomes partially firm (not stiff or it cannot be folded into milk mixture.) Place saucepan in cold water to speed up this process.

Sprinkle a thin layer of graham cracker crumbs in an 8-inch square ungreased pan.

Pour ice cold evaporated milk into chilled bowl. Whip until stiff peaks form. Sprinkle lemon juice over the top and continue whipping until very stiff.

Fold pineapple mixture into the whipped milk. When thoroughly combined, gently pour into prepared pan. Level top and sprinkle remaining crumbs over.

Place in refrigerator for approximately one hour to become firm.

To serve, cut into portions, loosen sides and lift out with pancake turner.

Other fruit may be substituted. For example, strawberries and strawberry gelatin.

Nutritional Analysis (per serving)

Calories 156	Carbohydrates .... 30.8 g
Calories from fat 10%	Dietary fiber .... 1.15 g
Total fat .... 1.69 g	Cholesterol .... 1.25 mg
Protein .... 5.20 g	Sodium .... 131 mg

Ricotta Cheese Spread

PAMELA STEWART, SEATTLE

12 ¹/₄-cup servings

1 pint low fat ricotta cheese
¹/₂ red pepper, minced
¹/₄ cup scallions, minced
1 small carrot, grated
1 clove garlic, minced fine
1 tablespoon fresh parsley, chopped fine
1 tablespoon fresh dill (or basil), chopped fine
1 tablespoon fresh lemon juice
1 tablespoon good olive oil
fresh ground pepper to taste
¹/₄ teaspoon salt

Mix all ingredients together in a bowl and taste for seasoning. Add more herbs if necessary. Chill in refrigerator about 1 hour before serving. Makes a great dip for raw vegetables or serve as a spread on whole wheat crackers.

Nutritional Analysis (per serving)

Calories 56.9	Carbohydrates .... 2.91 g
Calories from fat 50%	Dietary fiber .... .313 g
Total fat .... 3.22 g	Cholesterol .... 10.9 mg
Protein .... 4.19 g	Sodium .... 91.2 mg

Strawberry Treat Pie

LESLEE LOSEY, SPOKANE

Serves 8

Pastry

1 cup unbleached, presifted flour
¹/₂ teaspoon salt
¹/₄ cup canola oil
2 to 3 tablespoons cold water

Filling

32-ounce carton strawberry yogurt (low fat or nonfat)
1 large (8 serving size) package strawberry gelatin dessert mix
fresh strawberries, sliced

Stir salt into flour. Pour oil and cold water into measuring cup. Do not stir. Add all at once to the flour mixture. Stir lightly with a fork. Form a ball and flatten it slightly. Dampen table slightly. On table, roll dough ball between two 12-inch squares of waxed paper. When dough is rolled to edges of paper it will be the right thickness for crust. Peel off top sheet of paper and fit dough, paper side up, in a pie plate. Remove paper. Prick bottom and sides with a fork. Bake at 450 degrees for 10 to 12 minutes or until pastry is golden. Let cool.

Stir yogurt into a creamy consistency in a mixing bowl. Continue stirring while pouring the gelatin mix into yogurt. Pour mixture into cooled pie shell and refrigerate until serving. Garnish with fresh strawberries before serving.

Nutritional Analysis (per serving)

Calories 304	Carbohydrates .... 50.6 g
Calories from fat 24%	Dietary fiber .... 1.11 g
Total fat .... 8.25 g	Cholesterol .... 5.00 mg
Protein .... 8.38 g	Sodium .... 518 mg

Tartar Sauce

Selma Cole, Bothell

Serves 4

*1/2 cup nonfat plain yogurt
1 tablespoon corn oil
2 tablespoons sweet pickle, finely chopped
1 teaspoon onion, minced
1 clove of garlic, pressed
1/8 teaspoon dill weed*

Blend corn oil into yogurt. Add remaining ingredients and mix well. Serve with seafood.

Nutritional Analysis (per serving)

Calories 57.5	Carbohydrates .... 5.11 g
Calories from fat 54%	Dietary fiber .... 0.157 g
Total fat .... 3.51 g	Cholesterol .... 0.500 mg
Protein .... 1.73 g	Sodium .... 75.3 mg

Vegetable & Chip Dip

Kathy Rasmussen, Edmonds

Makes 8 1/4-cup servings

*2 quarts nonfat milk
1/4 cup buttermilk, nonfat or lowfat
salt or dried herb to taste, optional*

Heat milk to lukewarm over low heat. Pour into bowl. Stir in buttermilk. Cover and keep at room temperature for 24 to 48 hours or until a soft curd is formed and the mixture looks like a soft yogurt.

Line a colander with muslin or several layers of cheese cloth, set in sink. Pour in curd and let drain for about 10 minutes. Fold cloth over curd. Set colander on a rack over a rimmed baking pan, allowing about an inch between rack and pan bottom. Wrap entire unit with Saran wrap until air tight. Set in refrigerator to drain for 36 to 48 hours.

Spoon drained curd from cloth into bowl, stir in 3/4 teaspoon salt or dried herbs to taste. Discard whey accumulated in pan.

Makes about 2 cups of a soft, creamy cheese.

Nutritional Analysis (per serving)

Calories 45	Carbohydrates .... 2.85 g
Calories from fat 5.5%	Dietary fiber .... 0.008 g
Total fat .... 0.509 g	Cholesterol .... 4.28 mg
Protein .... 7.19 g	Sodium .... 45.5 mg

Yogurt Dip for Vegetables

Florence Tsukui, Seattle

Makes 8 2-tablespoon servings

*8 ounces low fat plain yogurt
1 1/2 teaspoons honey
1/2 teaspoon dry salad dressing mix
1 teaspoon salt-free dried herb and seasoning mix*

Mix ingredients well and let stand overnight in the refrigerator.

Nutritional Analysis (per serving)

Calories 22.0	Carbohydrates .... 3.09 g
Calories from fat 18%	Dietary fiber .... 0 g
Total fat .... 0.432 g	Cholesterol .... 1.75 mg
Protein.. .... 1.49 g	Sodium .... 19.9 mg

Yogurt Salad Dressing

Renée A. Kroese, Issaquah

Makes 16 2-tablespoon servings

*1 1/2 cups yogurt
2 tablespoons Dijon mustard
2 to 3 tablespoons honey
1/2 teaspoon garlic powder
fresh ground pepper and salt to taste
3 tablespoons nonfat milk
1 scallion
4 to 5 sprigs of fresh parsley*

Chop fresh washed scallion and parsley in food processor. Add remaining ingredients. Mix thoroughly. Refrigerate. If too thick add a little milk. If used for a dip, omit milk.

Variations: Add 3 to 4 teaspoons paprika powder, or add your favorite salt-free herb mix.

Nutritional Analysis (per serving)

Calories 27.2	Carbohydrates ....4.64 g
Calories from fat 15%	Dietary fiber ....0.068 g
Total fat ....0.470 g	Cholesterol ....1.57 mg
Protein ....1.36 g	Sodium ....41.3 mg

Yogurt Fruit Salad

KAREN T. DAMMANN, TACOMA

Serves 8

4 Granny Smith apples, chopped
³/₄ cup raisins
¹/₂ cup walnuts or any nuts, chopped
1 cup mozzarella cheese, diced
2 cups low fat vanilla yogurt, may substitute nonfat plain yogurt and add vanilla and sweetener

Mix ingredients together.

Nutritional Analysis (per serving)

Calories 257	Carbohydrates ....31.4 g
Calories from fat 35%	Dietary fiber ....2.97 g
Total fat ....10.3 g	Cholesterol ....17.8 mg
Protein ....12.1 g	Sodium ....190 mg

Beef, Pork & Lamb

Beef, Pork, & Lamb

Do you look longingly at the steaks and chops at the meat counter as you toss another package of chicken into your shopping cart? Take heart: Good health doesn't have to mean swearing off red meat forever.

There are three things to remember in order to make red meat a part of your low fat dietary plan: the cut, the method of preparation, and the amount per serving.

Let's look first at beef. The amount of fat in beef varies tremendously depending on the cut. Cuts lowest in fat and calories are those which include the words loin or round in the name. Tenderloin, top round steak (often called London broil), and triangle tip (also known as culotte steaks) are good examples of lean meats. A three-ounce, cooked, trimmed serving of top round steak has just 162 calories and 5.3 grams of total fat.

Different grades of meat affect the fat content, too. Marbling (the tiny streaks of fat you can see in the meat) is used by the U.S. Department of Agriculture to grade beef. Of the top three grades, Prime is the fattiest, followed by Choice and then Select.

Don't be afraid to include lamb and pork in your menus, either. Pork tenderloin, for example, is one of the leanest meats, with about 140 calories in a trimmed, cooked, three-ounce serving. But be careful. The same weight portion of pork sparerib meat has 340 calories.

Lamb's fat is mostly on the outside of the pieces and in layers between muscles, so it's important to trim away all visible fat before cooking. Lamb's calorie count for a three-ounce cooked serving ranges from about 155 calories for leg roasts to 235 for some chops.

But no matter how lean the cut you start with, you have to prepare it properly or you'll be adding fat and calories. Dieticians recommend the following preparation tips to "keep lean meat lean":

◆ Trim away all visible fat.

◆ Cook the meat quickly, on a high temperature setting.

◆ Broil, barbecue, or roast on a rack to allow fat to drip away.

◆ Marinate with spices, wine, lemon, or tomato juice instead of oil.

◆ Cook soups, stews, chili, and spaghetti sauces a day before and refrigerate. Skim off any hardened fat before reheating.

◆ Plan on four ounces of uncooked meat for every three-ounce cooked serving.

◆ Use a non-stick skillet to avoid adding extra cooking fat. Remove the drippings as they accumulate.

It's also helpful to adjust your thinking about what makes up a typical meal. Meat does not have to be the focal point of the dinner plate. Try looking at it as a condiment, rather than as an entree. Include larger portions of vegetables and salad and add a three-ounce serving of meat as an accent. Or try stir-frying a small portion of lean red meat with a generous mound of fresh vegetables.

The three-ounce servings recommended by dietitians may look small to "meat-and-potato" eaters accustomed to servings three times this size. But keeping those servings small is the key to keeping your meal low-calorie and low fat. A three-ounce serving of sirloin steak contains a relatively innocent 177 calories. Multiply that by three and you've got a 531-calorie nutritionists' nightmare. So enjoy red meat—but in small, carefully selected and prepared portions.

The following recipes may inspire some creative ideas for giving red meat a new role in your health-conscious diet.

Abby's Oriental Salad

ABBY ADAMS, BELLEVUE

Serves 4

³/₄ pound flank steak
2 tablespoons of teriyaki sauce mixed
*   with 2 tablespoons of water*
juice of 1 lemon

Salad

¹/₂ head leafy lettuce
¹/₂ head fresh spinach
2 carrots, shredded
3 stalks celery, sliced
¹/₂ cup bean sprouts
1 small can sliced water chestnuts
¹/₂ red or yellow pepper, sliced

Dressing

1 teaspoon sugar or honey dissolved in 2
*   teaspoons hot water*
2 tablespoons salad oil
¹/₂ teaspoon sesame oil
2 tablespoons wine vinegar
³/₄ teaspoon garlic, chopped
1 teaspoon low sodium soy sauce
2 cups crisp chow mein noodles

Marinate meat in teriyaki sauce and lemon juice for 3 hours in refrigerator. Broil on a charcoal grill or in the oven until cooked on each side. Cool and slice into bite size pieces. Prepare all salad vegetables and place in large salad bowl. Combine salad dressing ingredients in a small bowl. Just before serving add meat, salad dressing, and noodles to salad and toss together.

Nutritional Analysis (per serving)

Calories	493	Carbohydrates	59.9 g
Calories from fat	27%	Dietary fiber	8.34 g
Total fat	15.6 g	Cholesterol	63.3 mg
Protein	33.7 g	Sodium	553 mg

Cabbage Roll Stew

BARBARA SCHMITZLER, AUBURN

Serves 8

1 medium head cabbage
1 pound lean ground beef
1¹/₂ cups bread crumbs
¹/₂ cup skim milk
¹/₂ cup onion, chopped
¹/₄ cup dried parsley
¹/₄ teaspoon ginger
pepper to taste
nutmeg to taste
1 15-ounce can low sodium stewed tomatoes
1 can low sodium tomato sauce
4 medium carrots
4 medium potatoes

Parboil cabbage 3 to 5 minutes. Drain water and cool. Mix together ground beef, bread crumbs, milk, onions, parsley, ginger, pepper and nutmeg. Form into medium meat balls. Wrap each ball in cabbage leaf. Cover bottom of pan with stewed tomatoes. Place cabbage rolls in pan. Peel carrots and potatoes. Cut carrots in quarters and potatoes in half and place around cabbage rolls. Cover with tomato sauce. Bake in covered pan for 1¹/₂ to 2 hours at 350 degrees.

Nutritional Analysis (per serving)

Calories	362	Carbohydrates	53.2 g
Calories from fat	23%	Dietary fiber	7.23 g
Total fat	9.54 g	Cholesterol	38.2 mg
Protein	18.1 g	Sodium	618 mg

Chafing Dish Meat Balls

MARY ELLEN RUSHFELDT, TACOMA

Serves 4

1 pound lean ground choice beef
2 tablespoons onion, minced
1 teaspoon garlic, minced
2 tablespoons green pepper, finely chopped
¹/₄ cup corn meal
1¹/₂ teaspoons dry mustard

1 teaspoon hot chili powder
$^1/_4$ teaspoon salt
$^1/_2$ teaspoon pepper
$^1/_2$ cup milk
1 egg, beaten

Sauce

1 8-ounce can low sodium tomato sauce
1 teaspoon hot chili powder

Combine all the ingredients except for the sauce and form into 30 or 40 small balls. Roll in flour. Brown in a non-stick skillet, using a small amount of vegetable oil. Combine sauce ingredients and add to meatballs. Simmer about 45 minutes. Pour into chafing dish and serve with toothpicks.

Nutritional Analysis (per serving)

Calories	298	Carbohydrates	8.40 g
Calories from fat	56%	Dietary fiber	1.37 g
Total fat	18.4 g	Cholesterol	129 mg
Protein	24.7 g	Sodium	249 mg

Chashaoboas
(Roast Pork Buns)

H. LEUNG, SEATTLE

Makes 20 buns

Filling

3 cups roast pork, diced
2 tablespoons safflower oil
2 cups onion, diced
1$^1/_2$ cups chicken broth
Salt and pepper to taste
$^1/_4$ cup cornstarch

Dough Balls

2 cups all purpose flour
3 cups pastry or cake flour
1 teaspoon salt
$^1/_2$ cup granulated sugar
2 tablespoons baking powder
1 tablespoon active dried yeast
1 tablespoon sugar
2 cups warm water (90 degrees from the tap)

$^1/_4$ cup vegetable shortening
1 cup pastry or cake flour (dusting)

For filling, heat the wok or saucepan with oil, stir fry onion for 2 minutes. Mix in diced pork, chicken broth, salt and pepper. Bring to simmer. Stir in starch to thicken. Cool in refrigerator before using.

For dough balls, blend flours, salt, $^1/_2$ sugar and baking powder. Put aside. Put the one tablespoon sugar in the warm water. Sprinkle yeast into water and stir. Let stand 3 minutes. Mix in flour and stir. Add shortening last. Use extra cake flour to dry and knead the dough for 5 minutes. Cover and let ferment 3 hours.

To assemble, divide the fermented dough into 20 pieces. Form them into dough balls. Rest 15 minutes. Flatten the dough balls and fill them with 2 tablespoons roast pork filling. Seal at the top. Place filled dough balls on a square sheet of waxpaper. Arrange them in a steamer. Rest 30 minutes. Steam cook vigorously 10 to 12 minutes.

Or place filled dough balls smooth side up. Brush top with beaten egg. Rest 30 minutes. Arrange on a greased baking pan. Bake for 8 minutes at 375 degrees. Then broil 7 to 10 minutes to brown.

Nutritional Analysis (per serving)

Calories	226	Carbohydrates	34.5 g
Calories from fat	23%	Dietary fiber	1.26 g
Total fat	5.78 g	Cholesterol	13.5 mg
Protein	8.01 g	Sodium	204 mg

Chile Verde

Deborah Fausti, Olympia

Serves 6

1 cup white great northern beans
2¹/₂ cups water
¹/₈ teaspoon salt
2 cups fresh tomatillos
1 pound pork meat, cubed in ¹/₂ inch size,
*   trimmed of all fat*
1 medium onion, chopped
3 cloves garlic, chopped
1 anaheim (mild) chili pepper, chopped
1 jalapeno or serrano (hot) chile pepper,
*   chopped*
1¹/₂ teaspoon cumin
¹/₈ teaspoon salt
1 handful fresh coriander (cilantro leaves,
*   chopped)*
juice of ¹/₂ lemon

Bring beans, water and ¹/₈ teaspoon salt to boil in saucepan. Turn off heat and let sit until beans have swollen (about 1¹/₂ hours). Then cook over medium heat until tender, keeping just covered with water. Meanwhile peel tomatillos, add water barely to cover, and cook until soft, about 20 minutes.

Sauté pork, onion, garlic, and peppers in ¹/₄ cup of bean water until meat is brown and onion is soft. Add beans and tomatillos. Add enough bean and tomatillo water just to cover. Simmer. Add cumin and ¹/₈ teaspoon salt. Cook until meat is tender and flavors have mixed (at least ¹/₂ hour). Skim fat.

Add coriander and lemon juice 10 minutes before serving. Serve with warm flour tortillas.

Nutritional Analysis (per serving)

Calories 297	Carbohydrates .... 29.8 g
Calories from fat 26%	Dietary fiber .... 8.87 g
Total fat .... 8.80 g	Cholesterol .... 44.7 mg
Protein .... 25.3 g	Sodium .... 263 mg

Chinese Beef & Broccoli

Peggy Einzig, Seattle

Serves 4

1 pound thinly sliced flank steak, cut into
*   4-inch long strips*
2 large bunches fresh broccoli, steamed
*   soft, thinly sliced*
1 package (2 ounces) dried stemless shitake
*   mushrooms*
2 tablespoons low sodium soy sauce
4 teaspoons sugar
2 teaspoons cornstarch
3 tablespoons peanut oil
1 each, low sodium beef and chicken bouillon
*   cubes*
1¹/₂ cups boiling water

Pour about 1¹/₂ cups boiling water over mushrooms in ceramic bowl and let soak.

Mix meat, both mashed bouillon cubes, soy sauce, 2 teaspoons sugar, and cornstarch in bowl.

Drain mushrooms, which should now be soft, and slice thin, saving juice. Add mushrooms to meat mixture, stirring well.

Cook prepared broccoli in large hot oiled skillet at low heat 3 minutes, stirring once or twice. (Use peanut oil.) Remove broccoli from pan and return to bowl, adding dash of salt and 2 teaspoons sugar.

Sear meat mixture in hot oiled pan, about 5 to 7 minutes. Add broccoli, strained liquid from mushrooms and cook 1 to 2 minutes.

Serve with steamed rice.

Nutritional Analysis (per serving)

Calories 282	Carbohydrates .... 18.9 g
Calories from fat 34%	Dietary fiber .... 3.89 g
Total fat .... 10.8 g	Cholesterol .... 70.3 mg
Protein .... 28.5 g	Sodium .... 342 mg

Easy Lo-Cal Beef & Bean Casserole

CLARE LINCOLN, WOODINVILLE

Serves 6

2 medium onions, sliced
2 celery stalks, sliced
3 medium potatoes, sliced
1 teaspoon Worcestershire sauce
1 13-ounce can kidney beans, drained
2 tablespoons parsley, chopped
2 tablespoons green peppers, chopped
pepper and herb seasoning to taste
1 pound uncooked lean ground hamburger,
   crumbled
¹/₃ cup uncooked rice
1¹/₂ cup beef low sodium stock
dash of garlic powder to taste.
1 can low sodium tomato soup

Layer onions, celery and potatoes in large casserole. Mix Worcestershire sauce, kidney beans, parsley, green peppers, herbs, hamburger, rice, beef stock and garlic powder. Add to casserole.

Pour tomato soup over mixture. Cover casserole and bake about 2 hours at 300 degrees.

Nutritional Analysis (per serving)

Calories	389	Carbohydrates	50.3 g
Calories from fat	27%	Dietary fiber	8.12 g
Total fat	11.7 g	Cholesterol	49.6 mg
Protein	21.6 g	Sodium	410 mg

Fiesta Chowder

CAROL HARRIS, REDMOND

Serves 6

1¹/₄ cup dried pinto beans
1 pound lean pork loin chops
2 tablespoons safflower oil
1 cup onion, finely chopped
2 garlic cloves, minced
1 can low sodium tomato soup
4 cups water

2 teaspoons chili powder
¹/₂ teaspoon oregano
¹/₂ teaspoon cumin
¹/₄ teaspoon pepper
4 cups carrots, thinly sliced
1 7-ounce jar baby corn on the cob

Cover beans in water, boil for 2 minutes. Cover and let steam away from heat for 1 hour, drain. Trim meat and cut in ³/₄ inch cubes. Brown in oil. Add onions and garlic and cook until soft. Add beans, soup, water and spices. Cover and simmer 1 hour or until almost tender. Add carrots and corn, simmer 30 minutes more. Add water if needed. Garnish with cherry tomato halves, chopped cilantro, or fresh salsa.

Nutritional Analysis (per serving)

Calories	468	Carbohydrates	54.9 g
Calories from fat	28%	Dietary fiber	17.3 g
Total fat	15.0 g	Cholesterol	59.8 mg
Protein	30.9 g	Sodium	307 mg

Flank Steak

MARVEL D. GORDON, SEATTLE

Serves 4

1 pound flank steak
1 onion, chopped
dash of salt substitute and pepper
1 broccoli stalk, cut into strips, blanched
1 carrot, cut into sticks, blanched
¹/₄ pound mushrooms, sliced
¹/₄ cup Dijon mustard.

Butterfly flank steak. Spread open on table. Spread mustard, vegetables and seasonings on one side and roll up like a jelly roll. Tie and bake approximately 30 minutes at 375 degrees until medium rare or as desired.

Nutritional Analysis (per serving)

Calories	231	Carbohydrates	7.26 g
Calories from fat	36%	Dietary fiber	2.65 g
Total fat	9.23 g	Cholesterol	81.0 mg
Protein	29.7 g	Sodium	391 mg

Ground Beef & Vegetable Casserole

CAROL & MEENA MYKRIS, SEATTLE

Serves 6

1 pound lean ground beef
1 large dry onion, chopped
1 clove garlic, minced
1 tablespoon dry parsley
1 teaspoon garlic powder
1 eggplant medium size, sliced ¹/₂-inch thick
1 zucchini medium size, sliced ¹/₂-inch thick
3 potatoes, sliced ¹/₂-inch thick
1 tablespoons oregano
1 15-ounce can low sodium tomato sauce
1 tablespoon dry dill
¹/₂ cup Parmesan cheese

Brown ground beef, add chopped onions, minced garlic, parsley, oregano and dill. Add tomato sauce and bring to a boil, then simmer for five minutes.

Layer sliced potatoes in a 9-x-13-inch pan and spoon little of the meat sauce over it. Next, layer the sliced zucchini and spoon a layer of the meat sauce over it. Next, layer the sliced eggplant and cover with the rest of the meat sauce.

Sprinkle the Parmesan cheese on top evenly and bake in a preheated oven for 45 minutes at 375 degrees.

Nutritional Analysis (per serving)

Calories 332	Carbohydrates .... 32.3 g
Calories from fat 38%	Dietary fiber .... 6.49 g
Total fat .... 14.4 g	Cholesterol .... 55.9 mg
Protein .... 20.2 g	Sodium .... 204 mg

High Protein Meatloaf

AGNES JEAN WOOD, SEATTLE

Serves 8

1 cup each of three of these grains: Millet,
*   buckwheat, cracked wheat, wheat germ,*
*   wheat bran, oatmeal*

1 cup skim milk
2 eggs
2 pounds lean ground beef
1 tablespoon Worcestershire sauce
¹/₂ cup chopped onion
1 cup grated carrot
¹/₂ teaspoon salt
¹/₈ teaspoon pepper
¹/₄ cup parsley

Mix well. Put into a greased loaf pan. Bake one hour at 350 degrees.

Nutritional Analysis (per serving)

Calories 355	Carbohydrates .... 20.8 g
Calories from fat 46%	Dietary fiber .... 4.82 mg
Total Fat 18.8	Cholesterol .... 127 mg
Protein .... 28.0 g	Sodium .... 178 mg

Italian Beef & Vegetable Kabobs

JULIE GOLDING, SEATTLE

Serves 4

1 pound lean steak, cut into 1-inch chunks
1 large sweet onion, cut in 1-inch pieces
1 large sweet pepper, cut in 1-inch pieces
¹/₂ pound fresh mushrooms
2 small Japanese eggplants, cut in 1-inch
*   pieces*

Marinade

4 tablespoons light olive oil
¹/₂ cup red wine
1 teaspoon dried or fresh rosemary, crushed
1 teaspoon fresh parsley, minced
1 teaspoon fresh or dried thyme, minced
2 cloves garlic, crushed
1 teaspoon grated orange rind
dash Tabasco sauce
1 teaspoon fresh ground pepper
¹/₄ teaspoon salt (optional)

Mix all the marinade ingredients together in a large glass bowl and add the steak chunks. Marinate at least 4 hours, turning occasionally.

Thread kabob skewers with alternate

chunks of meat and vegetables. Brush kabobs lightly with the reserved marinade. Grill over a medium hot fire (or broil in oven) for about 10 to 15 minutes. Baste with marinade once or twice. Serve with rice, garnish with fresh parsley.

Nutritional Analysis (per serving)

Calories 262	Carbohydrates .... 10.9 g
Calories from fat 43%	Dietary fiber .... 3.77 g
Total fat .... 12.7 g	Cholesterol .... 65.0 mg
Protein .... 26.9 g	Sodium .... 63.7 mg

Jerry's Pork Roast "Louisiana Style" ⭐

JERRY JACKSON, BREMERTON

Serves 8

1 tablespoon red pepper flakes
3 tablespoons creole seasoning
2 whole green bell peppers, chopped
4 stalks of celery, chopped
2 tablespoons parsley flakes
1 clove garlic, peeled
2 cups white vinegar
1 pork roast, 2 to 4 pounds, bone removed

Chop and add vegetable ingredients together with vinegar and mix well. Let stand for a few minutes.

Make two inch slices in roast. Make holes about two inches deep and stuff roast with vegetables. Make as many holes as possible and stuff well. Pour remainder of stuffing evenly over roast.

Bake for 25 minutes at 400 degrees. Check and baste, bake 30 minutes at 350 degrees or until top is brown. Do not add water while baking.

Nutritional Analysis (per serving)

Calories 334	Carbohydrates .... 6.23 g
Calories from fat 48%	Dietary fiber .... 1.18 g
Total fat .... 17.8 g	Cholesterol .... 101 mg
Protein .... 36.4 g	Sodium .... 354 mg

Judi's Tasty Microwave Meatloaf

J. SCHWARZ, SEATTLE

Serves 6

3 slices bread, crumbled
1 small onion, chopped
1 stalk celery, chopped
2 egg whites
1 clove garlic, pressed or chopped
1¹/₂ pounds extra lean ground beef
4 to 5 tablespoons dijon mustard
¹/₈ to ¹/₄ cup chopped parsley
¹/₄ to ¹/₂ cup teaspoon whole fennel seeds
¹/₂ teaspoon paprika
¹/₂ teaspoon oregano
¹/₂ teaspoon basil
pepper

Mix all ingredients together (hands work best).

Put into microwave proof pan. Use a round casserole and shape the mixture into a doughnut for more even cooking.

Microwave for 20 minutes on high (100 percent). Rotate once or twice during cooking if not using a carousel.

Optional: Pour ¹/₄ cup catsup or tomato sauce over the top after 15 minutes of cooking.

Nutritional Analysis (per serving)

Calories 295	Carbohydrates .... 10.7 g
Calories from fat 52%	Dietary fiber .... 1.16 g
Total fat .... 17.2 g	Cholesterol .... 74.0 mg
Protein .... 24.4 g	Sodium .... 292 mg

Lamb Curry

SUSIE DADE, SEATTLE

Serves 6

1 pound lean lamb, cut into ¹/₂-inch chunks
1 large onion, sliced
3 large tomatoes, seeded and chopped
3 cloves garlic, minced

1 tablespoon of fresh ginger, peeled and
   minced
$^1/_4$ cup dry roasted unsalted cashews, ground
1 red bell pepper, chopped
2 tablespoons fresh curry powder, medium
   hot or light
$^1/_2$ cup vegetable or chicken broth
2 tablespoons fresh cilantro, minced
2 tablespoons olive oil
$^3/_4$ cup low fat plain yogurt
$^1/_2$ teaspoon salt
3 cups cooked rice

In large skillet, sauté garlic, ginger, and
onions in oil until soft and golden. Add
curry powder and cook on low heat for
about 5 minutes, stirring frequently to
prevent sticking. Add tomatoes, pepper,
broth and cashews and cook another 10
minutes.

Add lamb and cook on low heat for 1
hour, covered, until tender. Stir
occasionally. Remove pan from heat and
let cool for 5 minutes. Gently stir in
yogurt, cilantro and salt. Re-heat slowly
until hot and bubbly.

Serve over rice with such condiments as
sliced bananas, toasted almonds and
coconut, sautéed onions and cucumber
in yogurt.

Nutritional Analysis (per serving)

Calories	352	Carbohydrates	38.1 g
Calories from fat	32%	Dietary fiber	3.06 g
Total fat	12.4 g	Cholesterol	52.5 mg
Protein	22.2 g	Sodium	311 mg

Lamb Stuffed Zucchini

KAULEE DEAN, DES MOINES

Serves 4

4 zucchini
1 pound lean ground lamb
1 tablespoon catsup
2 tablespoon dried bread crumbs
$^1/_2$ teaspoon salt
$^1/_4$ teaspoon garlic powder

$^1/_2$ teaspoon Worcestershire sauce
$^1/_8$ teaspoon pepper
2 egg whites
1 tablespoon fresh grated Parmesan cheese

Cut off ends of zucchini and cook in
boiling salted water until slightly tender
(approximately 5 minutes). Plunge into
cold water, drain. Cut in half lengthwise
and scoop out pulp, leaving the shell at
least $^1/_4$ inch thick. Set aside. Mash or
finely chop zucchini pulp and add lamb,
bread crumbs, catsup, Worcestershire,
garlic powder, salt, pepper and egg. Mix
lightly, heap into zucchini shells,
arrange in shallow baking dish. Sprinkle
with cheese. Bake, uncovered, for 30
minutes or until well browned on top at
350 degrees.

Nutritional Analysis (per serving)

Calories	204	Carbohydrates	6.46 g
Calories from fat	33%	Dietary fiber	1.83 g
Total fat	7.43 g	Cholesterol	76.4 mg
Protein	27.3 g	Sodium	391 mg

A Lean Way to Enjoy Pork

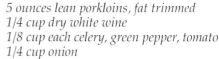

AMY A. SCHOONOVER, BENTON

Serves 4

5 ounces lean porkloins, fat trimmed
1/4 cup dry white wine
1/8 cup each celery, green pepper, tomato
1/4 cup onion
1 garlic clove
1 tablespoon capers, drained and rinsed
1 tablespoon lemon juice
1 teaspoon low-cal margarine
1/4 teaspoon thyme
Pinch of salt & pepper.

Cut pork into 1-inch strips. Mince
celery, green pepper, tomato and garlic.
Brown pork strips in large skillet, and
drain off excess oil. Add all other
ingredients and reduce heat to simmer
for 15 to 20 minutes.

Nutritional Analysis (per serving)

Calories 110	Carbohydrates .... 1.53 g
Calories from fat 50%	Dietary fiber .... .29 g
Total fat .... 5.95 g	Cholesterol .... 37.4 mg
Protein .... 11.9 g	Sodium .... 42.7 mg

Marinated Beef & String Beans

RUTH M. RUTTON, BAINBRIDGE

Serves 4

1 pound round steak, thinly sliced
2 tablespoons oil for browning steak
2 cups cooked rice

Marinade

4 tablespoons low sodium soy sauce
2 teaspoons sugar
2 tablespoons cornstarch
¹/₂ pound fresh string beans, cut into
*   1-inch lengths*
¹/₄ cup water
1 dozen french sliced mushrooms or 1 small
*   can of canned mushrooms*

Coat the sliced beef with marinating mixture and let stand from 1 hour to eight hours or overnight. (Longer makes meat more tender.) Steam string beans until tender. Heat a pan with oil and when hot, add meat and brown for 1 minute or more. Add the beans, water and mushrooms. Also add any remaining marinade mixture. Cover, turn down and let simmer 3 to 5 minutes. Serve immediately over rice.

Nutritional Analysis (per serving)

Calories 363	Carbohydrates .... 34.2 g
Calories from fat 27%	Dietary fiber .... 2.30 g
Total fat .... 10.8 g	Cholesterol .... 81.0 mg
Protein .... 31.0 g	Sodium .... 392 mg

Mediterranean Lamb Salad

STEPHEN SPENCER, SEATTLE

Serves 4

3 to 4 ounces lamb loin chops, trimmed
olive oil
garlic
1 teaspoon chili powder
1 teaspoon cumin
1 teaspoon oregano
pinch of rosemary
2 cloves garlic, minced
2 tablespoons red wine
¹/₂ cup onion, thinly sliced
¹/₂ cup yellow pepper, thinly sliced
¹/₂ cup carrot, thinly sliced
¹/₂ cup tomato, thinly sliced
¹/₂ cup fresh mint, chopped
cilantro, chopped
green onions, chopped

Rub lamb with olive oil and garlic. Grill and set aside.

In mortar/pestle prepare chili powder, cumin, oregano, rosemary, garlic, and red wine.

Thinly slice lamb. Place in bowl, add spice mixture, and toss. Add onion, yellow pepper, carrots, tomatoes, and mint. Mix.

On a plate place a few romaine lettuce leaves to one side. Cover rest of plate with torn bib lettuce. Place lamb mixture on top and garnish with cilantro and sliced green onion.

Nutritional Analysis (per serving)

Calories 77.5	Carbohydrates .... 5.53 g
Calories from fat 35%	Dietary fiber .... 1.58 g
Total fat .... 2.99 g	Cholesterol .... 19.9 mg
Protein .... 7.22 g	Sodium .... 33.8 mg

Mexican Picadillo Tacos

JOSEPH NELSON, SEATTLE

Serves 8

1 pound lean hamburger
¹/₂ medium onion, chopped
2 cloves garlic, minced
¹/₂ Granny Smith apple, chopped
2 large tomatoes, seeded, juiced and chopped
2 medium green chilies, seeded and chopped
¹/₂ jalapeno chili, seeded and chopped
¹/₂ cup raisins
1 tablespoon ground cumin
1 teaspoon chili powder
2 tablespoons fresh cilantro
¹/₂ teaspoon cinnamon
¹/₄ teaspoon ground cloves
¹/₄ teaspoon salt, optional
2 tablespoons vegetable oil
8 8-inch heated flour tortillas
topping of your choice: low fat yogurt,
*   lettuce, avocado, salsa*

Sauté onion, garlic and chilies in a large heavy skillet until soft and transparent. Add hamburger and sauté until no longer pink. Add tomatoes and cook on medium-low for about 5 minutes, then add the apples, raisins and spices. Cook over medium heat, stirring frequently for about 20 minutes. Adjust seasoning if necessary. Drain out any oil that may have accumulated. Serve as the filling for tacos with topping(s) of your choice.

Nutritional Analysis (per serving)

Calories	283	Carbohydrates	32.4 g
Calories from fat	37%	Dietary fiber	2.75 g
Total fat	12.2 g	Cholesterol	37.0 mg
Protein	14.0 g	Sodium	205 mg

Pork in Plum Sauce

SELMA COLE, BOTHELL

Serves 8

2 pounds lean boneless pork loin
1 tablespoon safflower oil
4 cups cooked rice
1 tablespoon toasted sesame seeds

Plum Sauce

1 pound can of whole purple plums in light
*   syrup*
1 medium sized onion, chopped
1 tablespoon low fat margarine
¹/₄ cup pure maple syrup
¹/₄ cup bottled low sodium chili sauce
2 tablespoons low sodium soy sauce
1 tablespoon fresh ginger root, grated
2 teaspoons lemon juice

Drain syrup from plums into a blender. Add plums after removing pits. Purée. Cook onions in margarine until limp. Add puréed plums and all other sauce ingredients. Simmer, uncovered for about 30 minutes, or until slightly thickened. Stir occasionally. Plum sauce can be made ahead of time. Will keep, refrigerated, for about one week.

Trim all fat from the pork loin. Cut it into one inch cubes. Heat oil in an electric skillet or large frying pan at medium high heat. Add pork cubes and brown on all sides. Drain off any remaining oil. Pour plum sauce over meat. Reduce heat to simmer. Cover. Cook 25 to 30 minutes, stirring occasionally, until pork is very tender when tested with a fork. Serve over rice, and garnish with sesame seeds.

Nutritional Analysis (per serving)

Calories	441	Carbohydrates	42.6 g
Calories from fat	32%	Dietary fiber	1.83 g
Total fat	15.6 g	Cholesterol	89.7 mg
Protein	31.0 g	Sodium	275 mg

Pork Tenderloin with Leek Sauce

STEPHEN SPENCER, SEATTLE

Serves 4

1 pound pork tenderloin
1 teaspoon olive oil
clove of garlic
1 teaspoon rosemary

Marinade

¹/₂ teaspoon black peppercorns
1 teaspoon Szechuan peppercorns
1 teaspoon cloves
¹/₂ teaspoon nutmeg
¹/₂ teaspoon thyme
¹/₂ teaspoon cinnamon
¹/₂ teaspoon oregano
¹/₂ teaspoon basil
2 bay leaves
¹/₂ teaspoon chili powder

Leek Sauce

2 leeks
¹/₂ cup onion, chopped
1 clove garlic
¹/₂ tablespoon margarine
¹/₂ tablespoon olive oil
¹/₄ cup or less white wine
parsley or cilantro for garnish

Rub tenderlion with olive oil, 1 clove garlic, and rosemary.

Grind marinade ingredients in mortar/pestle until well blended. Wrap marinade-coated tenderloin in plastic wrap and steam in steamer, approximately 30 minutes. This will seal in the juices.

For leek sauce, slice leeks and sauté with onion and minced garlic in margarine and olive oil. Reduce heat and simmer until soft. Purée and add a little white wine to correct consistency.

Slice pork. Place on plate, spoon sauce on. Garnish with parsley or cilantro.

Nutritional Analysis (per serving)

Calories	272	Carbohydrates	10.8 g
Calories from fat	46%	Dietary fiber	1.99 g
Total fat	13.5 g	Cholesterol	80.0 mg
Protein	25.3 g	Sodium	87.6 mg

Saucy Lemon-Dill Beef Strips

NANCY BREMERTON, SPOKANE

Serves 6

1 pound lean round steak
3 tablespoons low fat margarine
3 tablespoons flour
2 cups lowfat or skim milk
2 tablespoons lemon juice
1 tablespoon dill
¹/₂ teaspoon paprika
¹/₂ teaspoon garlic powder
¹/₂ teaspoon salt
dash of pepper
6 small fresh mushrooms, sliced
1 pound uncooked noodles

Cut beef into 1-inch narrow strips. Brown in skillet. Remove browned beef and dispose of dripping. Melt margarine in skillet; stir in flour until smooth. Add milk gradually; stirring constantly until sauce thickens. Add lemon juice, dill, paprika, garlic and pepper. Stir. Add beef strips and mushrooms to sauce. Cover. Simmer 30 minutes or until tender, adding water ¹/₄ cup at a time if sauce becomes too thick. Serve over noodles.

Nutritional Analysis (per serving)

Calories	409	Carbohydrates	43.3 g
Calories from fat	30%	Dietary fiber	3.68 g
Total fat	13.3 g	Cholesterol	103 mg
Protein	26.6 g	Sodium	232 mg

Spaghetti with Vegetable Beef Sauce

BOB HEFFERNAN, SEATTLE

Serves 6

¹/₂ pound extra-lean ground beef
2 teaspoons olive oil
1 medium onion, minced
2 cloves garlic, minced
¹/₂ cup celery, finely diced
¹/₂ cup carrots, finely diced
¹/₂ cup green pepper, finely diced
1 cup finely sliced mushrooms
1 28-oz. can plum tomatoes with juice
  or puree
1 6-oz. can tomato paste
1 tablespoon dried basil, crumbled
1 tablespoon oregano, crumbled
1 tablespoon crushed red peppers
¹/₂ teaspoon cardamon
several dashes cayenne, to taste
1 pound spaghetti
grated Parmesan

In a large skillet, lightly brown the beef. Remove beef with a slotted utensil to a plate lined with a paper towel. Clean pan and use it to heat oil briefly. Add onion and garlic and sauté about two minutes. Add celery, carrots, sweet pepper, and mushrooms and sauté for another minute.

Add tomatoes with their liquid, breaking them up as they go into the pan. Add tomato paste, basil, oregano, crushed red pepper, cardamon, cayenne, and beef. Bring to a boil over medium heat, reduce heat to low and let sauce simmer uncovered for about 30 minutes. Serve over cooked spaghetti. Sprinkle with Parmesan.

Nutritional Analysis (per serving)

Calories	345	Carbohydrates	50.6 g
Calories from fat	24%	Dietary fiber	6.35 g
Total fat	9.31 g	Cholesterol	27.3 mg
Protein	17.0 g	Sodium	334 mg

Sweet Roast Pork

CLEO KOCAL, SEATTLE

Serves 12

3 pounds pork loin
1 cup sweet wine
4 whole cloves
¹/₃ cup brown sugar
¹/₂ cup fine bread crumbs
¹/₈ cup low fat margarine
1 cup nonfat milk
¹/₂ teaspoon cinnamon
1 cup seedless raisins

Mix wine, cloves and brown sugar.

Trim all fat from pork

Add pork to wine mixture and marinate 6 hours.

Roll meat in bread crumbs. Dot with magarine. Put in roasting pan. Add rest of marinade to which you add milk, cinnamon and raisins.

Bake 35 to 40 minutes per pound at 325 degrees. Baste frequently.

Nutritional Analysis (per serving)

Calories	338	Carbohydrates	19.1 g
Calories from fat	37%	Dietary fiber	.90 g
Total fat	13.8 g	Cholesterol	107 mg
Protein	33.7 g	Sodium	140 mg

Sweet & Sour Meatballs

NETTIE E. ALMQUIST, EVERETT

Serves 8, 5 meatballs each

Meatballs

1¹/₂ pounds extra lean ground beef
²/₃ cup 1% milk
1 cup oatmeal
¹/₂ cup onion, chopped
¹/₄ tablespoon garlic powder
¹/₂ teaspoon salt
¹/₄ teaspoon pepper
1 egg

Sauce

1 cup catsup
³/₄ cup brown sugar
¹/₄ teaspoon garlic powder
¹/₄ cup chopped onion

Mix all meatball ingredients, shape into small balls and place in a flat pan or jellyroll pan. Mix sauce ingredients together and pour over meatballs. Bake for 1 hour at 350 degrees. May add water while baking.

Nutritional Analysis (per serving)

Calories 327	Carbohydrates .... 33.8 g
Calories from fat 36%	Dietary fiber .... 1.29 g
Total fat .... 13.3 g	Cholesterol .... 82.4 mg
Protein .... 18.8 g	Sodium .... 613 mg

Spicy Stir-fried Pork & Spinach

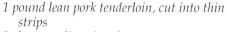

JULIE ROOS, BENTON CITY

Serves 4

1 pound lean pork tenderloin, cut into thin strips
2 cloves garlic, minced
2 tablespoons low sodium soy sauce mixed with 2 tablespoons of water
1 teaspoon red pepper flakes
¹/₂ medium sized onion, sliced into thin strips
2 10-ounce packages frozen cut leaf spinach, thawed, excess moisture squeezed out

Combine pork, garlic, soy sauce and pepper flakes and marinate 10 to 15 minutes.

Heat oil in wok or large skillet, until very hot. Add onions and pork. Cook, stirring constantly, until done. Add spinach and cook until heated through, stirring constantly. Serve over brown rice or whole wheat noodles.

Nutritional Analysis (per serving)

Calories 245	Carbohydrates .... 11.2 g
Calories from fat 35%	Dietary fiber .... 4.09 g
Total fat .... 9.75 g	Cholesterol .... 80.0 mg
Protein .... 29.7 g	Sodium .... 400 mg

Surprise Stew

SANA GLASSBURN, MARYSVILLE

Serves 4

¹/₂ pound hamburger, lean, browned and drained
1 onion, medium, sliced
1 turnip
1 parsnip
1 rutabaga
6 to 8 mushrooms
16 ounce can stewed tomatoes and juice
¹/₂ cup water
¹/₄ cup Worcestershire sauce
¹/₂ teaspoon oregano
¹/₄ teaspoon pepper
1 bay leaf

Slice vegetables, mix with fried hamburger, stewed tomatoes and juice, water, worcestershire sauce and spices in crockpot or microwave casserole. Cook in crockpot all day on low, 2 to 3 hours on high or in microwave 10 to 15 minutes on high, until vegetables are tender.

Nutritional Analysis (per serving)

Calories 198	Carbohydrates .... 18.9 g
Calories from fat 38%	Dietary fiber .... 5.19 g
Total fat .... 8.73 g	Cholesterol .... 37.0 mg
Protein .... 13.7 g	Sodium .... 413 mg

Vitello Tonatto Lighto
(Veal with Tuna Sauce)

STEPHEN SPENCER, SEATTLE

Serves 4

4 4-ounce veal steaks/cutlets, trimmed of fat,
*   pounded flat*
1 tablespoon olive oil
1 tablespoon rosemary
2 cloves garlic

Tuna Sauce

2 anchovies
juice of 1 lemon
¹/₄ cup stock veal or chicken, unsalted
¹/4 cup lowfat plain yogurt
3 ounces tuna packed in water, drained

Rub veal steaks with oil, garlic and rosemary. Grill and set aside. Don't overcook.

For tuna sauce, soak anchovies in water for 10 minutes. Remove from water and chop. Puree together with rest of sauce ingredients.

Set veal on plate, spoon some sauce over the veal and garnish with italian parsley and thinly sliced lemon, and if desired, a few drained capers and sliced olives.

Nutritional Analysis (per serving)

Calories 232	Carbohydrates ....2.44 g
Calories from fat 32%	Dietary fiber ....0.184 g
Total fat ....7.88 g	Cholesterol ....132 mg
Protein ....36.1 g	Sodium ....255 mg

Vegetables

▲▲▲▲▲▲▲▲▲▲▲▲▲▲▲▲▲

Vegetables

Did you grow up thinking vegetables were something that came out of a can and occupied the smallest space possible on a dinner plate? Fortunately, all that's changed. New research and nutritional education tell us that whether you want to lose weight, lower cholesterol, prevent cancer, decrease sodium, or lower fat intake, vegetables play a key role.

Fresh vegetables are low in calories, low in sodium, high in fiber, low in fat, dense in nutrients, and provide that full, satisfied feeling from their volume and bulk, says GHC dietitian Karen Redelf.

Fresh leafy greens are excellent sources of fiber and vitamin A. Fresh broccoli, cauliflower, and cabbage have been shown to lower cancer risk. Fresh squash and potatoes provide complex carbohydrates and important fiber.

But to get the most from these and other vegetables, you've got to pay attention to the word "fresh." Vegetables pack the healthiest punch in their most natural state, immediately after harvest. The longer they are out of the garden and the more they are cooked and processed, the more nutrients are lost—so plan your menus accordingly.

Include raw vegetables in your diet daily: Add shredded carrots or sliced cucumbers to sandwiches or have carrot sticks as a snack. Try cole slaw made with a low fat yogurt dressing.

When you do cook vegetables, use the smallest amount of water possible and cook them quickly. Steaming works well and so does the microwave. Both methods preserve the water-soluble nutrients, including vitamin C. Strive for that crisp-tender stage, not the soft mush.

Be a discriminating shopper when buying vegetables. Simply shopping in the fresh produce section of the supermarket doesn't ensure freshness. Be wary of wilted or bruised produce, signs that it's been too long since harvest. It helps to shop often. Vegetables lose nutrients in your own refrigerator as well as in the store.

If you can't get fresh vegetables, frozen is better than canned, says Redelf. You get less sodium and, because vegetables are usually frozen shortly after harvest, you get more nutrients.

▲▲▲▲▲▲▲▲▲▲▲▲▲▲▲▲▲▲

Be careful not to add your own sodium and fat to vegetables by way of sauces and seasonings. Skip the hollandaise. Go easy on the butter and margarine. Experiment with herbs as seasonings, including garlic, dill, parsley, mint, rosemary, basil, allspice, red pepper flakes, cilantro, marjoram, chives, and nutmeg. If you stir-fry, use a minimal amount of oil, or better yet, try a bit of bouillon or a non-stick pan.

Finally, if you want to get more vegetables into your diet, try to change the way you think about them. Start by promoting them from the lowly rank of a side dish you prepare with little creative thought. Instead, make one or two meals a week in which vegetables are the stars, not the supporting players. Redelf offers these tips:

◆ Experiment. Read the vegetable section of your favorite cookbook. Exchange recipes with friends. Don't assume that the way you've always prepared and served vegetables is the only way to go.

◆ Make this the year you and your family learn about vegetables you've never tried before. Introduce one new vegetable a week.

◆ Increase the ratio of vegetables when you're cooking your favorite stews or casseroles. In many cases you can double the amount of vegetables to lower fats and calories and boost the nutritional value.

◆ Add "bonus" vegetables such as lettuce, cabbage, carrots, sprouts, celery, green peppers, and cucumbers when you're preparing sandwiches, green salads, egg or tuna salads.

In addition to a healthier diet, there's one more good reason to increase your vegetable intake: your food budget will get a real shot in the arm. If you doubt it, make a trip to the store and visit only the produce department. You'll be amazed at the volume of food—and the good nutrition—you'll get for your money.

Asparagus with Red Peppers & Pine Nuts

DEBORAH RITCHEY, SPOKANE

Serves 4

1 red pepper, seeded and chopped
2 tablespoons pine nuts
2 cloves garlic, pressed or minced
3 teaspoons olive oil
2-3 tablespoons red wine vinegar
   (according to taste)
1¹/₂ to 2 pounds asparagus, fibrous ends
   removed, washed but leaving some
   moisture on the spears
freshly ground black pepper to taste

Brown pine nuts over medium heat, in large skillet, approximately 1 to 2 minutes, stirring frequently. Remove from skillet and set aside.

Add 2 teaspoons olive oil to skillet, then add garlic and red pepper. Sauté 2 to 3 minutes until pepper is tender-crisp, stirring occasionally. Add red wine vinegar and remove from skillet, set aside (keeping warm).

Add the remaining 1 teaspoon olive oil to skillet, then add asparagus spears. Cover. Cook 5 to 7 minutes (depending on thickness of spears) until tender-crisp, shaking skillet occasionally to stir.

Remove asparagus to serving dish, sprinkle with freshly ground pepper. Pour red pepper mixture across the asparagus spears and sprinkle on pine nuts.

Nutritional Analysis (per serving)

Calories 114	Carbohydrates .... 9.70 g
Calories from fat 50%	Dietary fiber .... 3.00 g
Total fat .... 7.46 g	Cholesterol .... 0 mg
Protein .... 7.21 g	Sodium .... 4.05 mg

Asparagus with Tomato & Blue Cheese

DEBORAH RITCHEY, SPOKANE

Serves 4

3 green onions, chopped
1 large tomato, seeded and chopped
3 cloves garlic, pressed or minced
¹/₃ cup dry white wine
3 tablespoons blue cheese, crumbled
1¹/₂ to 2 pounds asparagus, fibrous ends
   removed; washed but leaving some
   moisture on spears
3 teaspoons olive oil

Over medium heat in large skillet, add 2 teaspoons of olive oil. Add green onions and garlic, and sauté 1 minute. Turn up heat to medium high and add wine, reduce liquid by one half. Add tomatoes and cook until heated through. Remove from skillet and set aside, keeping warm. Reduce heat to medium.

Add the remaining 1 teaspoon olive oil to skillet, and then add asparagus. Cover. Cook 5 to 7 minutes (depending on thickness of spears) until tender crisp, shaking skillet occasionally to stir.

Remove asparagus to serving dish, pour tomato mixture across spears and sprinkle blue cheese over mixture. Serve immediately.

Nutritional Analysis (per serving)

Calories 108	Carbohydrates .... 10.1 g
Calories from fat 45%	Dietary fiber .... 3.48 g
Total fat .... 6.02 g	Cholesterol .... 5.24 mg
Protein .... 6.44 g	Sodium .... 108 mg

The Best Zucchini

RUTH BAAETZ AND
SANDRA JO PALM, SEATTLE

Serves 4

4 cloves garlic, minced
1¹/₂ pounds zucchini, sliced
1 teaspoon canola oil

2 teaspoons lemon thyme
2 tablespoons mirin*

Sauté garlic in canola oil in a non-stick frying pan. Add the zucchini and lemon thyme and stir fry until the zucchini is as tender as you like it. Just before serving, add the mirin and stir.

Note: If using plain thyme, add some tarragon.

*If you are unfamiliar with this ingredient, it is a sweet cooking rice wine available in most supermarkets in the soy sauce section.

Nutritional Analysis (per serving)

Calories 24.8	Carbohydrates .... 3.10 g
Calories from fat 42%	Dietary fiber .... 0.763 g
Total fat .... 1.28 g	Cholesterol .... 0 mg
Protein .... 0.910 g	Sodium .... 2.15 mg

Braised Fennel

PHIL S. DUVAL, ESPANOLA

Serves 6

1 tablespoon vegetable oil
2 garlic cloves, minced
3 cups fennel, sliced
1/2 cup water
1 packet instant low sodium broth and
*   seasoning mix*
1 teaspoon basil leaves
1/4 teaspoon pepper

In a small non-stick skillet heat oil. Add garlic and sauté until golden. Add fennel and sauté over medium heat, stirring occasionally, for 2 to 3 minutes. Add water, broth mix, basil and pepper and bring to a boil. Reduce heat and let simmer until fennel is tender, about 15 minutes. Serve hot.

Nutritional Analysis (per serving)

Calories 30.7	Carbohydrates .... 2.12 g
Calories from fat 67%	Dietary fiber .... 0.718 g
Total fat .... 2.42 g	Cholesterol .... 0.100 mg
Protein .... 0.509 g	Sodium .... 205 mg

Broccoli Quiche

(without the crust)

ROSE BALLEN, VASHON

Serves 6

1 pound broccoli, washed and cut into small
*   flowerettes, with stems cut into*
*   approximately 3/4-inch pieces*
1 medium onion, coarsely chopped
1/2 cup egg substitute
1 pint low fat cottage cheese
3/4 cup grated cheese (1/2 cup Swiss and
*   1/4 cup Parmesan combined)*
black pepper, basil, nutmeg to taste

Steam broccoli until tender but firm. Saute onion. In a bowl mix eggs, cheeses, vegetables. Add pepper and basil to taste. Spoon into a casserole prepared with a non-fat cooking spray, dust generously with nutmeg, and bake at 350° for 45 minutes.

Variation: Instead of broccoli, use one bunch spinach (chopped, cooked, and drained) or one package frozen chopped spinach (cooked and drained) and 1/4 to 1/2 pound fresh sliced, sautéed mushrooms.

Nutritional Analysis (per serving)

Calories 203	Carbohydrates .... 9.62 g
Calories from fat 38%	Dietary fiber .... 2.94 g
Total fat .... 8.70 g	Cholesterol .... 26.5 mg
Protein .... 22.2 g	Sodium .... 476 mg

Carrot Salad

SUSIE FRIEND, STEILACOOM

Serves 8

1 pound fresh grated carrots
1/2 cup raisins, rinsed and drained
1/4 cup sunflower seeds

Dressing

1 cup tofu (soft)
3 tablespoons apple juice concentrate

2 tablespoons olive oil or salad oil
¹/₄ cup cider vinegar
1 tablespoon dried basil or tarragon. Use twice as much if using fresh herbs.

For dressing, put all in blender and blend together until creamy. Add a little salt if desired. Taste and if not tart enough add a little more vinegar or lemon juice. You will have dressing left over which can be used on other salads.

Mix salad together with about ¹/₄ cup of dressing and refrigerate for at least 1 hour.

Note: You can mix some mustard with the dressing and use it for potato salad or green salads.

Nutritional Analysis (per serving)

Calories 91.9	Carbohydrates ....15.4 g
Calories from fat 29%	Dietary fiber ....2.81 g
Total fat ....3.17 g	Cholesterol ....0 mg
Protein ....2.33 g	Sodium ....21.6 mg

Carrots with Coriander

JEAN POULTRIDGE, BOTHELL

Serves 4

1 pound carrots, sliced and steamed
¹/₂ teaspoon ground coriander
2 tablespoons dry sherry
black pepper to taste
1 to 2 tablespoons lemon juice

Combine carrots with coriander and sherry. Season to taste with black pepper and lemon juice.

Nutritional Analysis (per serving)

Calories 61.5	Carbohydrates ....12.6 g
Calories from fat 4%	Dietary fiber ....4.01 g
Total fat ....0.226 g	Cholesterol ....0 mg
Protein ....1.29 g	Sodium ....76.5 mg

Kate's Borscht

KATE HUNTER, SEATTLE

Serves 6

5 cups low sodium chicken broth
4 whole peeled tomatoes, quartered
3 large carrots, cut bite sized
4 medium beets, cut bite sized
2 cloves garlic, minced
4 new potatoes, cubed
¹/₂ head cabbage, chopped
¹/₈ teaspoon dried chili peppers
3 peppercorns
1 tablespoon blackstrap molasses
2 tablespoons chopped fresh cilantro
3 tablespoons tarragon vinegar
1 teaspoon dill seeds
1 bay leaf

Combine ingredients and bring to a boil. Simmer for two hours. Serve hot or chilled. May also be served with a dollop of yogurt or sour cream.

Nutritional Analysis (per serving)

Calories 109	Carbohydrates ....24.3 g
Calories from fat 5%	Dietary fiber ....4.59 g
Total fat ....0.629 g	Cholesterol ....0.833 mg
Protein ....3.53 g	Sodium ....42 mg

Linda's Country Potatoes

LINDA M. S. THOMAS, RENTON

Serves 4

1 tablespoon olive oil
¹/₄ teaspoon each of the following:
    dried rosemary
    dried thyme
    dried tarragon
    black pepper
¹/₂ cup celery, minced
¹/₂ cup fresh parsley, minced
    (or 1 tablespoon dried parsley)
2 green onions, minced
2 garlic cloves, minced
1 pound small (1 inch in diameter) red potatoes, sliced ¹/₄ inch thick

Evenly coat a large (10-inch to 12-inch) skillet with oil. Heat at a medium setting. When oil is warm, add vegetables and spices. After 2 to 3 minutes, add the potatoes, stirring lightly to coat potatoes with oil and vegetables. Cover and cook about 30 minutes over medium heat, stirring about every 10 minutes to keep potatoes from sticking in the pan. Serve immediately.

Nutritional Analysis (per serving)

Calories 163	Carbohydrates .... 30.8 g
Calories from fat 19%	Dietary fiber .... 3.55 g
Total fat .... 3.57 g	Cholesterol .... 0 mg
Protein .... 3.13 g	Sodium .... 25.9 mg

Lynn & Alice's Vegie-Rice Bake

LYNN BOHLMANN, SEATTLE

Serves 6

1 cup uncooked brown rice
¹/₂ large white onion, chopped
1 medium carrot, chopped
1 broccoli stalk, chopped
1 medium parsnip, chopped
5 medium mushrooms, chopped
1 medium zucchini, chopped
³/₄ teaspoon garlic powder
1¹/₂ teaspoons Italian seasoning blend
dash of pepper
1 can tomato paste
1 6-ounce can fruit juice (grape, apple or cranberry)
1 16-ounce can low sodium tomato sauce
1 tablespoon sesame oil
¹/₂ teaspoon caraway seeds
³/₄ cup skim milk ricotta or
*   ¹/₃ carton chopped tofu*
8 cherry tomatoes, halved
³/₄ cup low fat mozzarella, grated

Cook 1 cup of brown rice in 1³/₄ cups water. Steam chopped vegetables with garlic powder, Italian seasonings, and pepper until crisp-tender. Put tomato

paste in medium bowl. Dilute with 1 can fruit juice and stir. Add tomato sauce and stir until blended. Set aside. Grease 10-inch square bake pan with sesame oil. Cover bottom of pan with rice. Sprinkle caraway seeds over rice. Dollop spoonfuls of ricotta or chopped tofu over rice. Spoon a thin layer of tomato sauce mixture over ricotta or tofu. Add steamed vegetables and cherry tomatoes. Pour remainder of tomato sauce mixture on top and stir lightly to coat vegetables. Top with grated cheese. Bake for 40 minutes at 375 degrees.

Nutritional Analysis (per serving)

Calories 322	Carbohydrates .... 45.0 g
Calories from fat 25%	Dietary fiber .... 7.35 g
Total fat .... 9.17 g	Cholesterol .... 24.5 mg
Protein .... 17.7 g	Sodium .... 257 mg

Mandarin Red Onion Salad

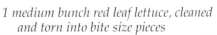

LYNDA PARRY, SPOKANE

Serves 4

1 medium bunch red leaf lettuce, cleaned and torn into bite size pieces
¹/₄ head lettuce, cleaned and torn into bite size pieces
1 medium red onion, cut in half and sliced
2 11-ounce cans mandarin orange segments, drained and chilled

Dressing

2 tablespoons olive oil
¹/₂ teaspoon sugar
1 tablespoon red wine vinegar
generous dash salt and pepper

Just before serving combine the salad ingredients and toss with red wine vinegar dressing.

Nutritional Analysis (per serving)

Calories 138	Carbohydrates .... 19.0 g
Calories from fat 43%	Dietary fiber .... 3.06 g
Total fat .... 7.11 g	Cholesterol .... 0 mg
Protein .... 1.81 g	Sodium .... 80.4 mg

Mardi Gras Vegetables

Ann M. Sires, Everett

Serves 6

1 16-ounce can low sodium Italian stewed
  tomatoes, broken up
$^1/_2$ small sweet onion, diced
$^1/_2$ each, red, green and yellow sweet peppers,
  cored, seeded and diced
1 large clove garlic, minced
$^1/_2$ cup cilantro, chopped
1 tablespoon fresh basil, chopped
  (or 1 teaspoon dry)
1 teaspoon fresh oregano, chopped
  (or $^1/_2$ teaspoon dry)
$^1/_2$ teaspoon fresh marjoram, chopped
  (or $^1/_4$ teaspoon dry)
1 cup low sodium tomato sauce
pepper to taste
2 each green and yellow zucchinis, cut into
  $^1/_4$" rounds

Add all ingredients except the zucchinis
and cilantro to a large sauce pan. Bring
to a boil, then turn heat and simmer for
10 minutes uncovered. Add zucchinis to
pot and cook, covered, until zucchinis
are fork tender. Sprinkle with cilantro.

Nutritional Analysis (per serving)

Calories 49.3	Carbohydrates .... 10.9 g
Calories from fat 8%	Dietary fiber .... 2.80 g
Total fat .... 0.519 g	Cholesterol .... 0 mg
Protein .... 2.59 g	Sodium .... 185 mg

Mediterranean Tomatoes

Kay Labitzke, Edmonds

Serves 4

1 pint cherry tomatoes
$^1/_3$ cup crumbled feta
1 teaspoon oregano

Place ingredients in bowl. Microwave
on high for 4 minutes. Serve.

Nutritional Analysis (per serving)

Calories 61.8	Carbohydrates .... 3.66 g
Calories from fat 57%	Dietary fiber .... 0.956 g
Total fat .... 4.19 g	Cholesterol .... 16.2 mg
Protein .... 3.51 g	Sodium .... 210 mg

Mexican Corn Salad

Laverne Kvilhaug, Seattle

Serves 6

1 16-ounce can whole kernel corn
1 chopped pimento
1 cup celery, diced
4 tablespoons sweet pickle, diced
$1^1/_2$ teaspoon chili powder
$^1/_4$ cup low fat mayonnaise

Mix chili powder with mayonnaise, add
other ingredients. Refrigerate for at least
8 hours before serving.

Nutritional Analysis (per serving)

Calories 116	Carbohydrates .... 22.4 g
Calories from fat 22%	Dietary fiber .... 5.04 g
Total fat .... 3.25 g	Cholesterol .... 2.67 mg
Protein .... 3.03 g	Sodium .... 153 mg

Orange & Red Pepper Potato Salad

Andrew Nelson, Bellevue

Serves 4

1 pound small new potatoes, unpeeled, cut
  into $^1/_2$ inch pieces
2 tablespoons olive oil
$^1/_2$ tablespoon red wine vinegar
3 scallions, chopped
$^1/_2$ cup red bell pepper, chopped
1 tablespoon fresh parsley, chopped
1 tablespoon grated orange peel
salt and fresh ground pepper to taste

Steam new potatoes until tender. When
still warm, toss with olive oil and
vinegar. Add vegetables and herbs and

toss again. Salt and pepper to taste. Serve at room temperature.

Nutritional Analysis (per serving)

Calories 165	Carbohydrates .... 24.5 g
Calories from fat 37%	Dietary fiber .... 2.19 g
Total fat .... 6.94 g	Cholesterol .... 0 mg
Protein .... 2.38 g	Sodium .... 139 mg

Outrageous Salsa

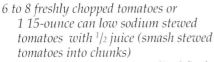

DEBORAH GALL, SEATTLE

Makes 32 2-tablespoon servings

*6 to 8 freshly chopped tomatoes or
1 15-ounce can low sodium stewed
tomatoes with $^1/_2$ juice (smash stewed
tomatoes into chunks)*
4 to 6 fresh jalapeno peppers, diced finely
4 to 6 fresh garlic cloves, diced small
*4 to 6 fresh green onions, diced thin,
including greens*
2 stalks fresh celery, diced fine
1 carrot, diced fine
1 green pepper, finely diced, optional
$^1/_2$ bunch fresh cilantro, finely chopped
$^1/_4$ teaspoon cayenne pepper
$^1/_4$ teaspoon cumin
salt and pepper to taste, optional

Combine all ingredients in bowl and store in refrigerator for approximately 1 hour or until chilled before serving.

Serve as a side dish with unsalted corn chips (tortilla chips) and fresh vegetable tray. Also great as accompaniment with eggs, tacos, burritos, etc.

Note: Some people may wish to use rubber gloves when dicing jalapeno peppers as they can burn the skin or any tiny cuts on hands or fingers.

Nutritional Analysis (per serving)

Calories 5.29	Carbohydrates .... 1.18 g
Calories from fat 8%	Dietary fiber .... 0.359 g
Total fat .... 0.055 g	Cholesterol .... 0 mg
Protein .... 0.233 g	Sodium .... 55.5 mg

Oven Baked Vegetables

CAROL AND MEENA MYKRIS, SEATTLE

Serves 6

1 teaspoon dry oregano
$^1/_4$ cup of vegetable oil
$^1/_2$ cup of lemon juice
*2 medium size zucchinis sliced $^1/_2$ inch thick
lengthwise, then cut into eight long cubes*
1 green pepper, sliced into $^1/_2$ inch thick slices
*3 medium carrots, cut into $^1/_4$ inch long
cubes*
1 large dry onion, sliced
3 cloves of garlic, minced
16 asparagus spears
25 sweet pea pods
1 tablespoon dry parsley
6 large mushrooms sliced

In a large baking pan (9-x-13-inch pan) place oil, garlic and dry onions and bake at 375 degrees for 10 minutes. Stir and then add in the carrots and lemon juice. Then add the zucchini, asparagus, green pepper and sweet pea pods. Bake for 10 minutes, stir frequently. Add in the mushrooms and then bake for 30 more minutes, stirring frequently. Vegetables should not be overcooked.

Nutritional Analysis (per serving)

Calories 173	Carbohydrates .... 19.3 g
Calories from fat 47%	Dietary fiber .... 5.74 g
Total fat .... 9.95 g	Cholesterol .... 0 mg
Protein .... 5.62 g	Sodium .... 21.2 mg

Red Slaw

NANCY DUNCAN, SEATTLE

Serves 6

1 medium head red cabbage, shredded
2 red Delicious apples, thinly sliced
1 red onion

Dressing

$^1/_3$ cup vegetable oil
$^1/_3$ cup cider vinegar
2 tablespoons sugar

1$^1/_2$ teaspoons celery seed
$^1/_8$ teaspoon pepper
1 cup plain nonfat yogurt

Combine salad ingredients. Combine dressing ingredients, stir until well blended. Toss dressing with salad.

Nutritional Analysis (per serving)

Calories 203	Carbohydrates .... 21.7 g
Calories from fat 53%	Dietary fiber .... 3.38 g
Total fat .... 12.6 g	Cholesterol .... 0.667 mg
Protein .... 3.72 g	Sodium .... 39.4 mg

Sautéed Spinach

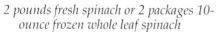

Joan Poultridge, Bothell

Serves 4

*2 pounds fresh spinach or 2 packages 10-
    ounce frozen whole leaf spinach*
2 cloves garlic
3 tablespoons olive oil
2 tablespoons raisins
2 tablespoons pine nuts, optional

Cook spinach until tender and drain well. Sauté garlic cloves in oil. When well browned, remove garlic, add spinach, turning frequently about 1 minute. Add raisins and pine nuts and sauté for another minute.

Nutritional Analysis (per serving)

Calories 193	Carbohydrates .... 13.5 g
Calories from fat 60%	Dietary fiber .... 8.03 g
Total fat .... 14.5 g	Cholesterol .... 0 mg
Protein .... 8.44 g	Sodium .... 179 mg

Scalloped Squash

Carmela Wilkins, Everson

Serves 6

*1$^1/_2$ pounds of butternut squash,
    cooked until tender*
1 onion, minced
1 clove garlic, minced
2 green peppers, chopped
2 tablespoons safflower oil

4 medium tomatoes sliced
a pinch of pepper on each slice
1 cup Parmesan cheese

Sauté onion, garlic and peppers in oil. Alternate squash, cooked vegetables, tomatoes and cheese in layers in greased casserole. Bake at 350 degrees until top is bubbly.

Nutritional Analysis (per serving)

Calories 181	Carbohydrates .... 19.8 g
Calories from fat 42%	Dietary fiber .... 5.34 g
Total fat .... 9.09 g	Cholesterol .... 10.5 mg
Protein .... 8.00 g	Sodium .... 264 mg

Slimslaw

Betty Brooks, Spokane

Serves 6

1 small head cabbage, slivered
2 small carrots, peeled, shredded
*1 15$^1/_4$-ounce can pineapple chunks in its
    own juice, drained, juice reserved*
*1 11-ounce can mandarin oranges in light
    syrup, drained*
3 tablespoons raisins
1 8-ounce carton plain nonfat yogurt
2 tablespoons pineapple juice
$^1/_4$ teaspoon nutmeg
$^1/_2$ teaspoon cinnamon

Combine and set aside: cabbage, carrots, pineapple, oranges, and raisins

Mix dressing: yogurt, pineapple juice and nutmeg and stir into above combined ingredients. Sprinkle with the cinnamon.

Nutritional Analysis (per serving)

Calories 129	Carbohydrates .... 30.6 g
Calories from fat 2%	Dietary fiber .... 4.02 g
Total fat .... 0.361 g	Cholesterol .... 0.666 mg
Protein .... 3.73 g	Sodium .... 51.4 mg

Slow Cooker Baked Beans

KATHLEEN HUECKSTEDT, SEATTLE

Serves 6

2 cups dry navy beans
$^1/_2$ cup molasses
$^1/_4$ cup honey
$^1/_4$ cup vinegar
1 tablespoon dry mustard
2 teaspoons low sodium soy sauce
1 8-ounce can low sodium tomato sauce
1 6-ounce can tomato paste
1 10$^3/_4$-ounce can low sodium chicken broth
1 medium onion, chopped fine

Wash beans, put into slow cooker and cover with 8 cups cold water. Cook at medium heat (#3 of 5 heat settings) for 12 hours. Drain water and discard.

If you have cooked the beans all day and are going to continue the next day, refrigerate beans overnight. Otherwise, just continue on:

Combine remaining ingredients and add to beans in slow cooker. Cook on low heat (#2 of 5 heat settings) for 12 hours.

If you can stir a couple of times during this period it helps to keep the ingredients well-distributed; but stirring is not really necessary.

Nutritional Analysis (per serving)

Calories	414	Carbohydrates	87.2 g
Calories from fat	4%	Dietary fiber	18.2 g
Total fat	1.75 g	Cholesterol	0.208 mg
Protein	18.9 g	Sodium	297 mg

Spicy Indian Green Beans

JOAN CATONI CONLON, SEATTLE

Serves 6

$^1/_2$ teaspoon mustard seeds
$^1/_2$ teaspoon cumin seeds

1 green chili, minced
1 to 1$^1/_2$ pounds green beans, chopped into inch-long pieces
$^3/_4$ teaspoon ground coriander
$^1/_2$ teaspoon ground cumin
$^1/_2$ teaspoon brown sugar substitute, optional

Spray non-stick pan with nonfat cooking spray. When hot, add mustard seeds. When they splatter, add cumin seeds and chili. Then add beans with a little water. Reduce heat and cover. When nearly done, add coriander, cumin and brown sugar.

Nutritional Analysis (per serving)

Calories	39.7	Carbohydrates	9.00 g
Calories from fat	5%	Dietary fiber	2.75 g
Total fat	0.245 g	Cholesterol	0 mg
Protein	2.30 g	Sodium	12.6 mg

Spicy Lentil Stew

LINDA LARSEN, ROCHESTER

Serves 6

1 cup dried lentils
2 cups water
8 ounces low sodium tomato sauce
1 32-ounce can low sodium tomatoes
1 clove garlic, minced
1 small onion, diced
2 carrots, thinly sliced
2 stalks celery, sliced
1 cup cooked lean ham, diced
1$^1/_2$ tablespoons chili powder
2 tablespoons parsely flakes
1$^1/_2$ teaspoons black pepper
$^1/_2$ teaspoon oregano

Rinse lentils thoroughly. Combine all ingredients and simmer in crockpot until lentils are tender, approximately 3 hours.

Nutritional Analysis (per serving)

Calories	216	Carbohydrates	34.2 g
Calories from fat	10%	Dietary fiber	9.54 g
Total fat	2.44 g	Cholesterol	12.8 mg
Protein	17.3 g	Sodium	341 mg

Steamed Ginger-Mint Carrots

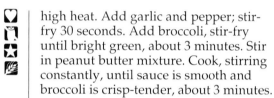

BARBARA HLAVIN, SEATTLE

Serves 4

1 pound carrots
2 1¹/₂-inch sprigs fresh mint
2 thin slices fresh unpeeled ginger root
lemon wedge

Peel carrots, or, if very young and tender, just scrub. Cut into 3-inch carrot sticks. Fill steamer basket with carrots. Fill pot to a depth of about 1¹/₂ inches with water. Put the mint and ginger in the water. Put the steamer basket in the pot. Bring to a boil. Steam for 2-5 minutes, depending on the age of the carrots. Immediately remove basket, dump carrots in serving bowl, and spritz lightly with lemon juice. Toss and serve. Decorate with a few fresh mint leaves or a sprig of mint.

Nutritional Analysis (per serving)

Calories 49.8	Carbohydrates ....11.7 g
Calories from fat 4%	Dietary fiber ....3.64 g
Total fat ....0.231 g	Cholesterol ....0 mg
Protein ....1.19 g	Sodium ....39.5 mg

Stir-Fry Broccoli with Spicy Peanut Sauce

CHRISTINE A. TURNER, SEATTLE

Serves 4

¹/₄ cup peanut butter, creamy if possible
³/₈ cup water
¹/₂ tablespoon low sodium soy sauce
1 teaspoon brown sugar
1 teaspoon vegetable oil
2 cloves garlic, minced
¹/₂ teaspoon crushed red pepper
4 cups sliced broccoli stems and
*   bite-sized flowerettes*

In small bowl, blend peanut butter, water, soy sauce and sugar; set aside. In a large non-stick skillet, heat oil over high heat. Add garlic and pepper; stir-fry 30 seconds. Add broccoli, stir-fry until bright green, about 3 minutes. Stir in peanut butter mixture. Cook, stirring constantly, until sauce is smooth and broccoli is crisp-tender, about 3 minutes.

Nutritional Analysis (per serving)

Calories 138	Carbohydrates ....9.09 g
Calories from fat 57%	Dietary fiber ....4.05 g
Total fat ....9.73 g	Cholesterol ....0 mg
Protein ....7.45 g	Sodium ....156 mg

Tofu Spinach Cannelloni

JOAN K. BABAD, RICHLAND

Serves 6

1 24-ounce box jumbo pasta shells

Sauce

1 32-ounce can pear tomatoes or
*   2 16-ounce cans low sodium whole*
*   tomatoes, chopped small*
2 8-ounce cans low sodium tomato sauce
1 medium onion, chopped fine
4 to 6 cloves garlic, chopped fine
1 teaspoon each dried oregano and basil

Pasta Shell Filling

1 10-ounce package of soft tofu, rinsed in
*   water and mashed fine*
1 cup Parmesan cheese
2 ounces egg substitute
2 10-ounce packages chopped spinach,
*   drained, water squeezed out*
¹/₂ teaspoon coarse ground pepper
1 teaspoon granulated dry garlic

1 12-ounce package mozzarella style cheese
*   substitute (soybean cheese), sliced thin*

Combine tomatoes, tomato sauce, spices, onion and garlic in deep saucepan. Simmer 30 to 45 minutes over medium heat to combine flavors. The sauce must be ready by the time you are ready to stuff the pasta shells.

Cook pasta shells for 7 to 9 minutes. Drain and cover with cold water until ready to fill.

Put filling ingredients in mixing bowl and mix well.

Prepare a 12-x-14-inch stainless steel baking pan with non-stick cooking spray. Put half the tomato sauce in pan.

Fill pasta shells with tofu/spinach mixture and place them in baking pan on sauce. Cut up any broken shells into ¼-inch slices to put over shells. Pour remaining sauce onto filled shells. Cover the pan with foil and bake for 1 hour at 350 degrees.

Remove foil and neatly arrange the sliced cheese substitute over the sauce covered shells. Return to oven and bake until cheese is melted and bubbly. The dish can be lightly browned under the broiler if desired.

Nutritional Analysis (per serving)

Calories	410	Carbohydrates	57.3 g
Calories from fat	22%	Dietary fiber	9.0 g
Total fat	10.7 g	Cholesterol	10.6 mg
Protein	26.8 g	Sodium	372 mg

Vegetable Lentil Salad

BYRDELLA EISENBARTH, NINE MILE FALLS

Serves 5

¹/₂ cup lentils
1¹/₂ cups water
¹/₄ teaspoon salt
1 cup cooked brown rice
¹/₂ cup bottled Italian dressing
    (oil free, low sodium)
¹/₂ cup tomatoes, diced
¹/₄ cup green pepper, chopped
3 tablespoons onion, chopped
2 tablespoons celery, chopped

Wash and drain lentils. Place in heavy saucepan; add water and salt. Bring to boil; then reduce heat and simmer, covered, about 20 minutes. Do not overcook. Lentils should be tender, with skin intact. Drain immediately. Combine them with cooked rice and pour dressing over mixture. Refrigerate until cool. Add remaining ingredients and mix well.

Nutritional Analysis (per serving)

Calories	136	Carbohydrates	24.7 g
Calories from fat	10%	Dietary fiber	4.22 g
Total fat	1.54 g	Cholesterol	1.40 mg
Protein	6.66 g	Sodium	301 mg

Vegetables Della Calabrese

ROBERT E. GIGLIOTTI, EDMONDS

Serves 6

2 tablespoons olive oil
1 medium onion, sliced, separate rings
2 cloves garlic, finely minced
3 medium zucchini, thinly sliced
5 Roma tomatoes, sliced
1 yellow bell pepper, chopped (may
    substitute red)
¹/₂ pound fresh mushrooms, sliced or
    quartered
8 ounces ripe pitted olives
2 or 3 pepperoncini peppers, finely chopped
2 tablespoons grated Parmesan cheese

Sauté onion and garlic in olive oil until glossy. Add zucchini and yellow pepper, sauté until nearly tender. Add remaining ingredients except cheese, continue cooking until tender. Garnish with cheese. Serve over rice or pasta or as a side dish.

Nutritional Analysis (per serving)

Calories	177	Carbohydrates	15.0 g
Calories from fat	61%	Dietary fiber	5.87 g
Total fat	14.2 g	Cholesterol	1.31 mg
Protein	5.06 g	Sodium	330 mg

Vegetable Souffle

Gertrude Leeds, Seattle

Serves 4

¹/₂ pound fresh vegetables (broccoli,
cauliflower, peas or whatever is in season)
1 tablespoon butter or margarine
1¹/₂ tablespoons flour
¹/₂ cup milk
¹/₄ cup grated Parmesan cheese
dash of pepper, nutmeg
2 eggs, separated

Cook vegetables in a small amount of water until about half done. Drain, reserving liquid. Arrange in the bottom of a greased 3-cup baking dish.

Melt butter, stir in flour, milk and 2 tablespoons of vegetable cooking liquid. Stir over medium heat until thick. Mix in cheese and spices. Cool a little, then beat in egg yolks. Whip egg whites until stiff and fold them into mixture. Spoon over vegetables in baking dish. Bake for 15 to 18 minutes at 400 degrees, until set in the center.

Nutritional Analysis (per serving)

Calories 110	Carbohydrates .... 7.07 g
Calories from fat 47%	Dietary fiber .... 1.54 g
Total fat .... 5.93 g	Cholesterol .... 109 mg
Protein .... 7.79 g	Sodium .... 185 mg

Vegetable Spaghetti Sauce

Mary Jordan, Poulsbo

Serves 6

2 14- to 16-ounce cans stewed low sodium
tomatoes
1 small can tomato paste
1 onion, chopped
2 carrots, finely grated
2 cups fresh mushrooms, sliced
³/₄ can water (stewed tomato can)
1 tablespoon Worcestershire
1 teaspoon oregano

dash garlic powder
pinch of red pepper flakes

Combine all ingredients and bring to boil. Lower heat and simmer 2 hours or more.

This sauce is even better if made one day and served next day. It is spicy and if a milder sauce is desired, omit red pepper flakes, reduce other spices to taste.

Nutritional Analysis (per serving)

Calories 87.4	Carbohydrates .... 19.2 g
Calories from fat 8%	Dietary fiber .... 5.24 g
Total fat .... 0.933 g	Cholesterol .... 0 mg
Protein .... 4.15 g	Sodium .... 337 mg

Zesty Veggie Salad

Charline Pearson, Olympia

Serves 6

2 medium broccoli stalks, tops cut off and
broken into small flowerettes,
1 medium zucchini, sliced thinly
2 small carrots, thinly sliced on the diagonal
1 green pepper, thinly sliced lengthwise (or
use a purple, red or yellow pepper)
large handful mixed sprouts
2 medium tomatoes, diced
1 7-ounce can artichoke hearts (not
marinated), quartered
3 tablespoons Romano cheese, freshly grated
2 tablespoons pine nuts, finely chopped
6 tablespoons lemon juice
¹/₂ teaspoon garlic powder
¹/₄ teaspoon basil
¹/₄ teaspoon oregano

Combine all vegetables in a large bowl. Sprinkle cheese and pine nuts over top.

Mix lemon juice with garlic powder, basil and oregano, add to vegetables and toss.

Nutritional Analysis (per serving)

Calories 99.5	Carbohydrates .... 14.4 g
Calories from fat 29%	Dietary fiber .... 6.85 g
Total fat .... 3.71 g	Cholesterol .... 2.95 mg
Protein .... 6.43 g	Sodium .... 82.5 mg

Zucchini-Carrot Salad

PATRICIA A. GONVERS, SEATTLE

Serves 4

2 cups zucchini, sliced thin
1 cup carrots, sliced thin
1/2 cup celery, sliced thin
4 tablespoons oil-free Italian dressing
1/4 cup green onion, sliced
1 cup tomato wedges
4 lettuce leaves, if desired
4 teaspoons sunflower seeds

Put zucchini, carrots and celery in a bowl and marinate with salad dressing for about 1 hour. Add green onion and tomato wedges and toss with other salad ingredients. Place 1 lettuce leaf in each of 4 salad bowls; put in salad and sprinkle top of each salad with 1 teaspoon sunflower seeds.

Nutritional Analysis (per serving)

Calories 67.3	Carbohydrates .... 10.5 g
Calories from fat 30%	Dietary fiber .... 3.48 g
Total fat .... 2.44 g	Cholesterol .... 0.875 mg
Protein .... 2.60 g	Sodium .... 164 mg

Zucchini-Carrot-Tomato Casserole

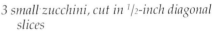

DYAN BLACK, MOUNTLAKE TERRACE

Serves 4

3 small zucchini, cut in 1/2-inch diagonal slices
3 large carrots, cut in 2-inch julienne strips, (2 cups)
1/2 pound cherry tomatoes, about a dozen
2 tablespoons cornstarch
1 1/2 cups nonfat milk
1 cup sharp cheddar cheese, grated (divide in half)
1/4 cup slivered almonds

Steam carrots until crisp-tender. Toss together carrots, zucchini and tomatoes in a 12-x-8-x-2-inch baking dish.

In a saucepan over medium heat stir cornstarch, milk, and 1/2 cup cheese. Stir until thickened. Pour over veggies and sprinkle with the rest of the cheese and the almonds. Bake for 30 minutes at 375 degrees or until zucchini is at the crisp-tender stage.

Nutritional Analysis (per serving)

Calories 267	Carbohydrates .... 21.2 g
Calories from fat 49%	Dietary fiber .... 4.72 g
Total fat .... 15.1 g	Cholesterol .... 33.5 mg
Protein .... 14.1 g	Sodium .... 248 mg

▲▲▲▲▲▲▲▲▲▲▲▲▲▲▲▲▲

Acknowledgements

Special thanks to those in the Group Health community who submitted more than 700 recipes to Simply Healthy and to those Group Health departments, employees, and volunteers who contributed to this project:

Automated Services Department; Nutrition Services, GHC Central and Eastside Hospitals; The Foundation for Group Health Cooperative; Group Health's "I'll Try Anything Once" volunteers; Dr. Don Rogers; Eileen Paul and Maureen Raskin, GHC nutritionists; GHC Take Care Stores; Public Relations Department; Group Health Northwest.

VIEW staff members: Christine Dubois, Jacqueline M. Hickey, Kristine Moe, Mary Rohrbach Robertson, Susan McElroy Plunkett, Mary Woodworth.

Members of the ACC Employee Health Promotion Team: Dorothy Talbot, Ginny Scobba, Debra Moore, Deborah Dickstein, Jody Kleven, Kristi Meuchel.

GHC Employee Test Cooks: Karen Artz, Caren Boland, Pat Cavin, Mary Colasurdo, Wanda Current, Joan DeClaire, Deborah Dickstein, Christine Dubois, Elisabeth Fredericksen, Susan Gardner, Nancy Gilbert, Wendy Graff, Barbara Hardman, Jacqueline M. Hickey, Jamie Hunter-Mitchell, Mary Jewell, Marge Jones, Colleen Judd, Suzanne Kaneda, Susan Kanvik, Erica Kay, Jody Kleven, Margot Kravette, Barbara Lardy, Sue Larson, Sharon LeVan, Jennifer Maeser, Barry McConnell, Meg McHutchison, Cindy McKinley, Kristi Meuchel, Kristine Moe, Lilly Moloney, Debra Moore, Wendy Noritake, Marianne Painter, Eileen Paul, Becky Peterson, Susan McElroy Plunkett, Mike Reandeau, Mary Rohrbach Robertson, Landa Rose, Linda Luano, Sharron Ruhlen, Carol Schlosnagle, Linda Schultz, Ginny Scobba, Gail Thompson, Bonnie Vaughn, Kyle Walsh, Mary White Peters, Christina Woeltz.

GHC Employee Taste-Testers.

▲▲▲▲▲▲▲▲▲▲▲▲▲▲▲▲

Thanks also to those businesses who contributed prizes for the Simply Healthy drawings:

Admiral Thriftway, The Ballard Market, Bumblebee Tuna, Central Co-op Grocery , Dairy Farmers of Washington, Domino's Pizza, Doug Fox Travel Agency, Gai's Bread, Kashi Cereal, Litehouse Salad Dressings, Market Spice Teas, The Meat Shop, Napoleon Olive Oil, Pasta and Co., Puget Consumers' Co-op, Starbuck Coffee, Sunkist Growers, Inc., The Sunlight Cafe, Sur La Table, The Take Care Store, Talking Rain, Uwajimaya, Washington Beef Commission, Washington Cheese Company, Queen Anne Thriftway, QFC Stores, Zenith Supplies.

Editorial Staff

Wendy Noritake, *Director, VIEW Publishing;*
Joan DeClaire, *Managing Editor;* Elisabeth Fredericksen,
Wendy Slotboom, *Copy Editors;* Carlene Canton, *Writer;*
Marianne Painter, *Production Manager;*
Margarite Hargrave, *Designer;* Gail Thompson, *Production;*
Margot Kravette, *Marketing Coordinator and NutritionalAnalysis;*
Mary Colasurdo, *Recipe Coordinator;*
Jacqueline Espinosa, *Data Entry;*
Karen Redelf, *Consulting Nutritionist;*
Evan Kentop, *Computer Programmer*

Index by Type of Dish

Salads

Side Dishes

Soups

Index by Subject & Title

YES! I would like to order additional copies of *Simply Healthy:*
A Collection of Favorite Recipes from the Group Health Community.

Name _____

Address _____

City _____ State _____ Zip_____

Please send me (number of copies) at $8.95 per book: _____

Add tax of $.72 per book: _____

Add shipping and handling of $1.30 per book: _____

TOTAL _____

Make checks payable to: The Foundation of Group Health Cooperative
Send to: GHC, VIEW Publishing, 521 Wall St., Seattle, WA 98121
Allow 4 weeks for delivery.

YES! I would like to order additional copies of *Simply Healthy:*
A Collection of Favorite Recipes from the Group Health Community.

Name _____

Address _____

City _____ State _____ Zip_____

Please send me (number of copies) at $8.95 per book: _____

Add tax of $.72 per book: _____

Add shipping and handling of $1.30 per book: _____

TOTAL _____

Make checks payable to: The Foundation of Group Health Cooperative
Send to: GHC, VIEW Publishing, 521 Wall St., Seattle, WA 98121
Allow 4 weeks for delivery.

YES! I would like to order additional copies of *Simply Healthy:*
A Collection of Favorite Recipes from the Group Health Community.

Name _____

Address _____

City _____ State _____ Zip_____

Please send me (number of copies) at $8.95 per book: _____

Add tax of $.72 per book: _____

Add shipping and handling of $1.30 per book: _____

TOTAL _____

Make checks payable to: The Foundation of Group Health Cooperative
Send to: GHC, VIEW Publishing, 521 Wall St., Seattle, WA 98121
Allow 4 weeks for delivery.